Edmund Neville, Trinity Cathedral in Newark

Gleanings Among the Wheat Sheaves

Sermons Preached at Trinity Church, Newark, N.J.

Edmund Neville, Trinity Cathedral in Newark

Gleanings Among the Wheat Sheaves
Sermons Preached at Trinity Church, Newark, N.J.

ISBN/EAN: 9783337159771

Printed in Europe, USA, Canada, Australia, Japan

Cover: Foto ©Lupo / pixelio.de

More available books at **www.hansebooks.com**

GLEANINGS

AMONG THE

WHEAT SHEAVES;

OR

SERMONS

PREACHED AT

TRINITY CHURCH, NEWARK, N. J.

BY THE

REV. EDMUND NEVILLE, D. D.

RECTOR.

—————————

NEWARK, N. J.

S. C. Atkinson, Printer, No. 1 New street.

· · · · · · · · · ·

1860.

TO

THE PEOPLE

OF

ST. THOMAS' CHURCH, TAUNTON; ST. PHILIP'S CHURCH, PHILADEL-

PHIA; CHRIST CHURCH, NEW ORLEANS; ST. THOMAS',

NEW YORK; AND TRINITY CHURCH, NEWARK,

These Sermons

ARE DEDICATED,

WITH GRATEFUL RECOLLECTIONS OF YEARS OF MINISTERIAL

LIFE PASSED IN THEIR SERVICE, BY

THE AUTHOR.

PREFACE.

THESE Sermons are published to comply with the frequently expressed wishes of many persons and for no other reason.—Should they be thought less favourably of in print, than they were in the pulpit, the Author can only remind his friends, that Elocution lends a grace even to what is feebly conceived, and illy expressed; and that perhaps their good opinion of his Sermons has been less owing to their composition, than to their delivery. They have been selected from many others, not because the Author attaches to them a special value, but because with few exceptions, they are on subjects in which all denominations of Christians are interested. Should they prove acceptable as a memorial to those with whom the writer has been officially connected, or should their perusal be attended with profit *to* others, the end of their publication will be fully answered.

Newark, August, 1860.

CONTENTS.

SERMON XIX.

THE NATURE AND BENEFITS OF CONFIRMATION.

Hebrews 6; 2.

"And of laying on of hands."

MINISTERIAL DIFFICULTIES.

" Who is sufficient for these things?"

II Cor. 2: 16.

THE ministerial office is lightly esteemed in the world, and little sought after; almost any other profession ranks higher in public sentiment. But if you look at the arduous duties which St. Paul assigns to clergymen, and read his account of the qualifications which they ought to possess, you will find that he regards their field of labour as worthy of the strong man's tillage; where the largest minds may range, and the loftiest imaginations soar. Ask him, and he will tell you that no man is equal of himself to discharge the duties of a minister; that they are "weighty enough," as Augustine says, " for Angel's shoulders." Such is the doctrine of the text, and coming here as I do,* to preach "Christ and him crucified," why may it not be useful to state the grounds of this doctrine? If there be any force in the Apostle's words, may I not expect your good will and sympathy, your indulgence and co-operation during what I hope will be a useful ministry? Does it not follow that you should make allowances, and not expect too much, when St. Paul says so plainly of a clergyman's duties, " Who is sufficient for these things?"

Let me, then, lay before you some of the difficulties he has to contend with. They are as grave and numerous now as ever they were. A minister of the nineteenth century, can ask the question in the text with as much justice as St. Paul could in the first.—

---

* Preached on taking charge of Trinity Church, Newark.

He has two kinds of difficulties to contend with; those which arise from himself, and those which arise from his office. He has *personal* difficulties, springing from his own nature, and *professional* ones, arising from the nature of what he has to do.

1.—First, with regard to his personal difficulties; here is *helplessness.* " Who is sufficient for these things ?" None of us can do any good without God's blessing. There is a blacksmith; he understands his business, and every blow that he strikes tells; but by mere force of words you can make no impression upon the human heart; try it at home upon your own children, at the Sunday School, or in the world—you will find that to attempt by words to conquer the heart is idle. A child might as well attempt to conquer a giant. I may preach in this pulpit for years, and leave no mark on the mass of my hearers. If only the human heart yielded as naturally to the Preacher's words, as iron to the hammer, every soul would be converted that heard him preach; but no such connexion exists between preaching and conversion. It may or may not be effectual as God pleases. In His hands, it is compared to a " hammer that breaketh the rock in pieces," but it altogether depends on Him to make it so. Do not expect me to change your hearts; I have not the power. Have not some of you heard the gospel preached for years without benefit? The Preacher has wielded the hammer of God's word, but so far as you are concerned, he has only beaten the air, or struck a blow on the natural feelings. It is only when God aims the blow, that it goes right home to the sinner's heart, and makes him cry out, " What must I do to be saved."

The Preacher is helpless. Very often he is taught this by being left a long time, for the trial of his faith, without seeing any fruit of his labours. Sometimes, by finding more good to result from sermons which cost him little pains, than from those on which he has expended all his strength; aye, by finding even a text of more avail than all he has to say about it. I remember a striking instance of this. Two men on their way to commit a crime were passing a church. They were house-breakers. "Go in," said one of them to his companion, "and see what hour it is." Now it pleased God, that the text announced as the man entered was, "Be sure your sin will find you out." The effect was electrifying; he was riveted to the spot. It was "hard" for him, as our Lord said to Saul, "to kick against the pricks." He could no more leave that church than the converted thief could leave the cross. What had the preacher to do with that? They were not his words, but those of God, that were made a blessing. Above all men, a minister has to remember that God is everything, and that he is nothing. His strength lies in feeling his weakness; and yet he must work all the while as though he depended on his own exertions. "Who is sufficient for these things?"

But there is *qualification* here. "Who is sufficient for these things" in point of *personal holiness*, for example? We not only want the strength, but the moral fitness which the work requires. We are naturally devoid of both. A minister must go to heaven by the same road as other people. He must be justified by faith in Christ first, and he must be sanctified by the Holy Ghost afterwards. He has to contend with the world, the flesh, and the Devil, and watch over the corruption of his nature, and the struggles of indwelling sin like yourselves; and oh! how hard is it for him oftentimes to keep fast hold of pious affections. Unless closely watched, holy feelings, like aromatic salts exposed to the air, evaporate.—Do you not find it so with yourselves? Is it not as much, and sometimes more than you can do to maintain your character as private soldiers in the army of Christ? But it is much harder for the commissioned officers than it is for you to be consistent. You are not always in regimentals, as we are. Many an officer has fallen because his uniform made him a mark for the enemy's riflemen.— There is a corps of slanderers in Satan's service, who find nothing to do but to shoot at the Ministers of Jesus Christ, and it is hard to bear. It stirs up our wrath to be calumniated and evil spoken of. You have heard, perhaps, that after the death of Archbishop Tillotson, a bundle of papers was found in his desk, on which was written, "These are libels; may God forgive their Authors; I do." Well, such a spirit is more readily admired, than imitated. As long as the "new man" has the mastery, when reviled he will not revile again; but if the "old Adam" gets the upper hand, the greatest Perfectionist living is apt to err.

Flattery endangers ministerial holiness, by raising conceit, almost as much as slander, by provoking wrath. A clergyman, being told on coming down from the pulpit, that he had preached a splendid sermon, replied that the Devil had whispered the same thing to him already.

> "O popular applause! what heart of man,
> Is proof against thy sweet, seducing charms!
> The wisest and the best feel urgent need
> Of all their caution in thy *gentlest* gales:
> But swelled into a *gust* — who then alas!
> With all their canvas set, and inexpert,
> And therefore heedless, can withstand thy power?"

I am paralyzed sometimes, when I think how much is expected of a Clergyman. His faults are descried as soon as stains on a white robe, spots on the sun's disc, or specks on the polished lens; and yet except he were exempt from human infirmities, he cannot always be influenced by divine affections. Still he must be holy, or lose his influence, mar his usefulness, and disgrace the Church. "He that will set the hearts of others on fire, must himself burn with love." Our Lord told Peter, "*After* thou art converted, strengthen thy Brethren;" which means, if I read it aright,

"He that would reform others, must be himself reformed." When I think on the excuses which people find for their remissness in our neglect, and how they cry out against religion itself on account of the inconsistencies of its friends, the importance of holiness to a minister of the Gospel is plain enough; still its difficulties are not obviated by its necessity. Is it an easy thing, my Brethren, with like passions as other men, to maintain such sweetness of temper, such fervour of spirit, and such prudence of speech, as shall make us "in word, in conversation, in charity, in faith, in purity," an example to believers? to be so amid annoying circumstances, trying cares, chilling disappointments, and depressing influences? Is it easy, when so much is expected of us, to "approve ourselves, as the ministers of God?"

You imagine, perhaps, that these difficulties are met by our professional employments; you say that they are so serious, bring us so often into the presence of God, and into scenes of distress, as must needs exert upon us a sanctifying influence, and be highly subservient to personal holiness. But, alas! they may have the opposite effect; the tendency of our doing anything habitually is to do it mechanically. Even laymen are in danger, through the constant use of the Prayer Book, of becoming formal, and our familiarity with sacred things may cause us to forget the concernment of religion with ourselves, and to fall into a heartless discharge of the most solemn duties. "Who is sufficient for these things?"

II.—And now, secondly, what *professional* difficulties has a clergyman to contend with?

With those of being a *faithful Preacher* in the first place, and a *useful Pastor* in the second. If it were easy to be faithful, St. Paul would not say so resolutely, "I am determined not to know any thing among you, save Jesus Christ, and him crucified." He saw great difficulties in the way of it, and set his face like a flint against them.

The fear of man is a difficulty. Many a one has fallen over that precipice. I shall not be here a month before Satan will be urging me to sacrifice truth to please my hearers. There is a man, he will say, for instance, who makes religion consist in punctilious adherence to outward observances. Preach up your own Church, and preach down all other Churches, and he will vote you a saint. Now let him alone, why should you offend his prejudices? Do not say to him, " Except thou art born again, thou canst not see the kingdom of God." Let him have his own way —. There is another who fancies that because baptized with water he is a new creature. If you undeceive him, and speak of the regenerating influences of the Holy Ghost, you will only incur his dislike, and lose the aid of his means and influence.—There is a third staid, sober, moral man, who " trusts in himself that he is righteous;" take care not to disturb his complacency with the doctrine of justification by faith alone.—And let those gay and worldly people enjoy themselves; darken not their sunny dreams with visions of death and judgment. " Speak unto them smooth things, prophecy deceits."

Satan is a great enemy to faithful preaching. " We are not ignorant of his devices." He suggests to us sometimes that the lower we put the standard for the people, the less we shall be criticized ourselves. Thou Arch Deceiver! What! set up a dwarfish model for the people that I may be a dwarf myself! Make them hug the shore because I fear to launch into the deep! No, rather will I hold up to them " the measure of the fulness of the stature of Christ" for a standard. Rather will I tell them to aim at the stars that they may shoot high, and to soar with the eagle, that they may approach the sun.

The fear of man is one of Satan's deadliest weapons. It resembles the poisoned robe which Dejanira gave to Hercules. The strongest man, once endued with it, becomes like Sampson when shorn of his locks, a weakling. Methinks that Satan in the shape of a polite gentleman wishes now to put that robe upon my shoulders. It will be such a help to you, he says, in a new parish, such a safeguard against excess and fanaticism. You refuse.—Ah, but he rejoins, you have literary and intellectual men among your hearers, who will not bear plain speaking. This will help you to new ideas, striking thoughts, and forcible arguments. You refuse again.—But listen; you have men of taste in your congregation, who will be offended with your homespun Saxon and blunt straightforwardness. Many of your hearers are practical men, this will qualify you to preach on the great topics of the day; they wish you to have something more modern than Gospel themes; they are musty, antiquated and behind the times. No, no! a hundred times no; I have always preached Christ, I will preach him again, I will preach him to the end, I will preach him only. Ah! my friends, but it is not always easy to say no. Interest, reputation and worldly considerations, will struggle with a minister's sense of duty, as well as with your own. Have you never been tempted to adopt what is expedient, rather than what is right in your own concerns? It is so with ourselves. Many inducements for a temporizing, politic and modified exhibition of the truth, are presented to our minds, and it requires great courage and faithfulness to do our duty. How hard is it to reprove, rebuke, exhort, with all long-suffering and doctrine; "not to be afraid of the words, nor dismayed at the looks of men," but whether they will hear, or whether they will forbear, to show them their transgressions and declare unto them their sin." "Who is sufficient for these things?"

Then again, it is not easy to preach in the *right way* in point either of style, or adaptation. The style of preaching that pleases now, is not that which pleased formerly, and although the truths of the Gospel never change, the method of preaching them must vary with the spirit of the age in which we live. We must take the thoughts of the old divines, and run them into moulds of modern taste. We must do with them as with the plate that used to adorn our fathers' sideboards; melt them down and put them into shapes of the latest fashions. Why should not the American Pulpit have a character of its own? Our habits and ways of thinking and forms of expression, are different from those of other countries. Our scenery, our customs and many objects proper for illustration because familiar to the people, are peculiar to ourselves; and I adopt the maxim that what is most intelligible to the hearer, is the most effective. The most intelligible style is that in which people converse every day of their lives. In place of the polished sentences, rounded periods and pointless smoothness of Blair's sermons which are "like fishing lines without hooks," we want a bold, simple and lively way of preaching, that is not afraid of compromising the dignity of the pulpit by an anecdote, or newspaper paragraph, or whatever may be instructive. The pulpit it is said is "dying of dignity," and we have to take off the ruffles which it wore in the days of Charles and the starched frills which it had on in the time of Elizabeth, and present it to the public in an American dress.

Then in respect to *adaptation*, regard must be had in preaching to the consciences as well as to the tastes of the people. We must so speak that they must hear a voice saying to them, "Thou art the man;" else what you intend for one may chance to be handed to another. I have often observed that persons are disposed to put the cap you wish them to wear themselves on the head of a neighbour, unless it be a very good looking cap which they need not be ashamed of; and it is difficult so "rightly to divide the word of truth," as to prevent their doing so. Then the professing members of a congregation, how far are they from being equally advanced in the divine life! Some are babes, some young men and some fathers in Christ. Is it not hard to determine what treatment is required by the diversities of their natural or Christian character, and to adopt towards them the address best suited to their respective circumstances? He is indeed "a workman that needeth not to be ashamed, who thus giveth every one his meat in due season." But no man will understand the difficulty of doing all this unless he has tried it. Our multifarious duties are the chief obstacle. So long as clergymen are expected to write more in a year than many authors do in a lifetime; make more speeches in one month, than some lawyers do in twelve; and as many visits as a physician; so long will they be obliged to say of a Preacher's duties, "Who is sufficient for these things?"

This brings me to notice the difficulty of being a *useful Pastor*, for preaching is only a part of our work. Preaching may be compared to the showers which water the whole field, but our other duties resemble the culture bestowed on each plant, and involve therefore a larger share of time and toil. There are family visitations for example. I think them very valuable as a means of promoting confidence and affection between Pastor and People; but at the same time too much of this kind of labour is often expected of a Clergyman. There are some persons who think that he should be a sort of perambulating machine, always on the move from house to house. Yes, but in that case, when is he to write his sermons? Let him preach his old ones. But if he does that, how shall he improve? We live and learn like other people. You expect more from a man of my age than you would from one ordained yesterday, but my old sermons represent me as I was formerly. Riper years have brought, as I hope, riper thought, wider knowledge and improved expression. We cannot afford to discard old sermons entirely, but neither am I prepared to rely upon them altogether. We must write new ones and we must have time for their preparation. A sermon is not written in a day.

Stimulated by that magical word of four letters, "Fame," in all its meanings, the public Lecturer expends weeks in preparing for his audience. Why should we do less for God than he does for

Gold? Why should I be expected to give less time to a sermon from which I expect a harvest of souls than he devotes to a lecture which he writes for Mammon? No; family visitation is highly important, but we have duties to perform of still more consequence; to improve our minds, to visit the sick and afflicted, to instruct the young, and to attend all our occasional services. And Oh! what care must be taken in discharging many of these duties, not unnecessarily to give offence and yet not to be deterred from faithfulness by the fear of offending. How hard is it when conversing with inquirers to detect self-delusion, to distinguish between the feelings of Nature and the work of the Spirit, not to "break the bruised reed, nor quench the smoking flax," but to administer just such counsel as the case requires.

Many of the Pastor's duties are painful and distressing. He is often called to see men who have lived wickedly in the world, until they can no longer enjoy it, and the prospect of death and judgment fills them with dismay. There lies the child of folly, so lately gay and thoughtless, now writhing under the lashes of an accusing conscience. Tossing from side to side on an uneasy pillow, he asks me how he may escape from the wrath to come. Is it not hard to deal with such sorrows? How difficult not to flatter the dying sinner with false confidences! How hard to withhold from him the consolations of religion, until he is the subject of repentance towards God, and faith in the Lord Jesus Christ! But above all, how difficult amid the perplexities and anxieties of our office and the distractions of other things, to maintain such a frame of mind, such a devotional spirit, as is essential to those who may be called at any hour, to the discharge of such solemn and affecting duties! "Who is sufficient for these things?"

Now, that I have sketched our difficulties, and shown you that they are insuperable by human strength, what shall we do with them, my Brethren? I think that the most of you will say,

" Our sufficiency is of God," let us cast the burden of them on the Lord. Well then, if we do that, it will be a good beginning, a firm foundation to build upon, for, "except the Lord build the house, they labour in vain that build it !"

> " In vain Apollos sows the seed,
>   And Paul may plant in vain,
> Till God the plenteous shower bestows,
>   And sends salvation down."

And what shall we do next? You would not have us imitate the man who, when his waggon wheels were clogged, contented himself with crying for help to Jupiter? Perhaps you say, " Oh no ! the *Minister* will put his shoulder to the wheel, and with God's aid will get it clear ;" but remember, God helps those who help themselves. Whatever degree of blessing may attend my labours in this parish will be small, compared to what we may expect from our united labours. What I ask of you then in view of ministerial difficulties, is first, *Prayer,* and secondly, *Exertion.*

Prayer,—This is the appointed means, and so a sure one, of being blessed. Clouds charged with blessing are floating over our heads, and prayer is the conductor that will bring it down. Prayer draws blessings, as Franklin's kite drew the lightning from heaven.— Money cannot purchase the Spirit's influences, but prayer secures his mighty aid. Some regard prayer as breath given to the winds. They will give anything to the Church but their prayers. I could mention church enterprizes that have probably failed from this circumstance. Large sums of money were bestowed on them but they might as well have been cast into the sea, because not given in the spirit of prayer. Now there are two or three hundred communicants, I am told, in this parish ; and if all of them will offer prayer before they go to rest to-night, that " the word of God may have free course among us and be glorified," it will augur well for our enterprizes; it will not be, my dear brethren, like the smoke of two or three censors rising upwards, but it will be a vast cloud of incense ascending to heaven from the censor of each member of the parish. May the Lord put it into your hearts to do this.

And as to the subjects of this prayer, I would say first, Pray for us Brethren; that I may be a faithful watchman for souls; ready to spend body, and mind, time and strength, in the work of my calling; and such a follower of the Lord Jesus myself as to be worthy of feeding the flock of which he has made me an Overseer.

Pray for *yourselves*, that you may be humble. penitent, spiritually minded, holy and zealous. If showers of grace are to descend on this parish, the Communicants must first feel their influence. The revival must begin with professing Christians. Beyond a doubt the most useful parishes that we have, are those distinguished by the zeal and piety of their members. It is not the words, but the deeds of professors which make an impression on the world. If we are a united, holy and active people, we shall attract the poor moths which flutter about every bright light that shines, and save souls that might perish otherwise.

Pray for the *neighbourhood*. There are a good many churches, I see, in this place, but the population is large enough to admit of their all doing good to the extent of their ability. I would have you pray that we may be made a blessing to those in our neighbourhood, who are not connected with any church at all, and who are living without God in the world. I do not wish to take a stray sheep from any other man's fold; but I should like to bring as many wanderers to the fold of Christ as possible. If we are Christians, we shall feel for the spiritual destitution of those who live at our own doors, who are like "sheep having no shepherd;" we shall have compassion on them and pray God to turn their hearts to us that they "may go in and out with us and find pasture."

Lastly, *Exertion.*—What I ask of you on this head is to be full of good works; to strive to give effect to all the agencies for promoting godliness that we may employ. There is our Sunday School, for example. I put that first, because I believe it to be in the very front rank among all the means of usefulness existing in the Church of Christ. Nothing can supply the want of early religious training. There is most danger to be apprehended in this country from the want of the religious education of children at home, than from any other single cause whatever, perhaps from all other causes combined; and the Sunday School is the only means we have of supplying the neglect of parents in this particular. What help may I expect from you in this department of Christian effort? We want teachers; how many of you, male and female, will come to our aid in the Sunday School? There is a young man who looks as if he might do good service. What does he say? He says that he works hard all the week. Yes; but whom do you work for? Myself—Exactly; then there is the more reason for your doing something for Christ on the Sabbath. Do you mean to apologize for being all day idle in the *Lord's* vineyard, by saying that you have been so busy in *your own?* Christ will say, Friend, did I not bid thee to go and work in *my* vineyard?—You will be classed among the wicked and slothful servants if you do nothing for Him, and everything for yourself.— There is an elderly person who would make a good teacher, but he says that he is too old. You are mistaken.—The fact of your being spared, plainly intimates that God has something more for you yet to do. When we can do no more good here, God takes us to himself, and we leave the earth, crying out with the Apostle Paul, "I have finished my course, I have kept the faith; henceforth there is laid up for me a crown of glory which God, the righteous Judge, will give me in that day." But it has not come to that with you yet. You have abilities and experience more mature now to serve God with, than you had formerly, and I tell you plainly that it is solemnly incumbent on you to employ them for Christ.

There are many other plans of usefulness which, by your aid, I hope to see set on foot among us, my dear hearers, and they will be spoken of when the time arrives for their execution. Let this suffice for the present. Only let us not be afraid of work. It is a good maxim, in and out of the Church, not to be afraid of work; but we hear it oftener from the lips of men of the world, than we do from the children of light. I would not attempt more than we can accomplish, but at the same time I would attempt all that we can reasonably hope to accomplish. Let us remember, that although no one of himself "is sufficient for these things," still that "we can do all things through Christ strengthening us."

THE CHESS PLAYERS.

2 Sam. 18: 29.

" Is the young man safe?"

These are David's words in regard to his son Absalom. Impelled by ambition, the young man had conspired against his father.— David was obliged to flee from Jerusalem, and defend his crown. After a battle between his troops, and the insurgents, the first question he asked referred to Absalom. "Is the young man safe?" But I mean to use these words apart from their connection on the page of history. I mean to ask generally, without alluding to any one in particular, "is the young man safe?" I remember seeing a picture called "the Chess Players." A young man was playing with one, who had not the features of a man at all. He looked more like the incarnation of evil than like a human being. His chin rested upon his bony hand, and his piercing eyes were fastened upon the youth, with such a malignant look, such an anxious gaze, such a hideous scowl, that years have not effaced from my memory the expression. I remember it still, and I have since thought that the painter might have improved his picture, by placing demons behind the chair of one of the players, and angels behind that of the other, all holding their breath, and watching with intense eagerness the progress of the game. The angels trembling lest the youth should make a false move, and the demons trembling lest he should make a right one. For this is the game of life. We and our Adversary the devil, are the players, and the stake is the soul.

Tremendous stake! No wonder that sympathizing angels descend from heaven to behold the contest.

> "Angels, whose radiant circle, height o'er height,
> Order o'er order rising, blaze o'er blaze,
> As in a theatre, surround the scene,
> Intent on man, and anxious for his fate."

It is in this sense that I use the language of the text. I speak of the soul. " Is the young man safe" under these circumstances? I shall endeavour to point out his dangers in the first place, and his only means of safety in the second; what he has to fear for defeat, and on what alone he must depend for success.

I. First then, he has much to fear from the *character of his opponent.* In proof of this, I need only mention a few particulars. Satan is not a *fair* adversary; that is the first point. There is always more to be dreaded from a faithless foe, than from an honourable one. A man of honour will take no undue advantage of his enemy, he will fight lawfully; but Satan has no scruples about what means he employs to destroy the soul. He will as soon make use of poison as of the sword; he will strike a man when asleep, or in the dark, just as readily as he would at noon day. Now, if with a gambler, a young man is sure of being victimized, what chance has he of success with such an adversary? The treachery of Satan, alone, is enough to enable us to predict the issue. Before a move is made on the board, it is easy to tell that the youth will be worsted in the unequal conflict. Besides *Satan is full of malicious and revengeful feelings.* A tiger robbed of its young is less savage than he who "goeth about like a roaring lion, seeking whom he may devour." He is exasperated by his fall from heaven. He is furious at the loss of the starry crown, and shining robes, and high place that once belonged to him. He was pitched headlong from the very pinnacle of glory, to the abyss of hell, and burns with rage against God. Does not this tend to aggravate the young man's peril? Satan knows what God has done for our salvation. He knows what tender solicitude he has evinced that we should not perish, and will he not be impelled by his enmity to God, to counteract, oppose, and thwart his purposes? Will he not make sure if possible, that the young man shall never join the ranks, and swell the praises of the redeemed. That no glory shall ever accrue to God from his devotion to his cause, his love of his name, and his zeal for his honour? That angels shall never sing the song of his conversion, nor bear to Jesus the incense of his praise? Besides, Satan is unable without pain to see us happy. His pride would be soothed by the young man's ruin. It would gratify his envious feelings to see him in the dust. Through grace he may escape perdition. He may obtain glory, honour, and immortality. He may even dwell in the very mansions which Satan, and his angels, once inhabited. The devil will prevent that if possible. Nothing excites his rage more than excellence, or happiness in another, and as envy made him conspire against Adam, so will it impel him to betray the young man into sin, and reduce him if he can to his own level. He has much to fear from this circumstance, the malignant envy of the devil. He is in danger likewise from Satan's *cunning*. The devil knows our weak points, and where we are most vulnerable. If, like Achilles, we could only be wounded in one spot, Satan would speedily discover what it was. Look at him in the wilderness when he tempted Christ. He went round about him like a general reconnoitering a fort to discover the best point of attack. Having taken Fort Adam, by assailing the bastions of pride, cupidity and ambition, he attempted to take Fort Emanuel in the same way. He was repelled; the artillery of heaven drove him off. But had not his adversary been invulnerable; had there been a flaw in his defences; Satan, we may be assured, would have found it out.—

The young man is in danger from the traps which from knowledge of his character Satan sets for him. They are often hidden. His profound cunning is never more evident than in concealing his game; and years sometimes elapse before a young man finds out that he is taken captive. By evil examples, pernicious books, or profligate companions, Satan sows the seeds of vices in his heart, and they take root without any one suspecting it, until in after life the disastrous tares make it manifest. Satan coils up a torpid serpent in the bosom of the boy, sure that it will be warmed into life, and activity, by the passions of the man. The train laid in the convivialities of earlier life, is fired subsequently. The harvest sown, perhaps, at sixteen, ripens at forty. Never underrate the danger of what are called the indiscretions of youth. You may think that ultimately no harm can spring from them. You may laugh at the first oath which a young man utters; you may call his sins, frolics; and speak of him as sowing his wild oats; but these are Satan's first moves on the chess board of life, and you might as well say that no consequences will arise from the first move of a fine chess player, as that the temptations to which a young man yields, will not tell injuriously upon him afterwards.

2. Secondly, he has much to fear from *himself.* Were there not in young men so much material for him to work upon, Satan would be less formidable. It is their ignorance, inexperience, and impetuosity. It is their impulsiveness, and pride, and vanity, that give him the advantage. Of all others, for instance they are most readily *deceived by appearances.* Of all others, they are slowest to suspect a snake in the grass, or a wolf in sheep's clothing; of all others, therefore, they are most likely to be imposed on by Satan in disguise. From this circumstance they are in awful danger of being led on to ruin; because, intimately acquainted with human

nature, Satan adapts his temptations to our respective foibles.—
Are you convivial?—He is straitway metamorphosed into a boon
companion. He says "draw the cork, fill the glass, sing the song."
Deceived by appearances, you call it harmless. After taking a
little, you propose to stop; but you take a little so often, that
you acquire a habit, you contract a disease, which recurs at last in
hourly paroxysms. You are poisoned; you have swallowed a snake;
your body swells; your face burns; your eyes redden; your health
fails; your limbs droop; and you sink, thread-bare and ragged into
the drunkard's grave. To those who are fond of social pleasures, this
is one of Satan's most fatal lures. How many young men we have
known to become its victims! They are deceived by appearances
and self conceit. There is the danger. They say, "we have a strong
will." So had Tiberius Cæsar, of whom Seneca says, "he was only
drunk once in his life; that was from the moment he became intoxicated to the day of his death." So had Alexander the Great;
who after conquering the world, perished by draining the cup of
Hercules. Woe be to him who contends with Satan in his own
strength. Again, are you *passionate?* Then Satan assumes another
form. Milton, after painting the snake in the brightest hues possible, reminds us, by making a toad whisper into the woman's ear,
that sometimes the loveliest forms are the most dangerous. He
says of the snake, "pleasing was his shape, and lovely," but by
placing a toad on Eve's shoulder, he reveals the object of Satan in
thus disguising himself. You know that a young man never sus-
pects the lurking of a toad in a comely form. Although he hears it
croak, and knows by his feelings that all his absorbents are imbibing
venom, yet by a charm like that of serpents upon birds he is so
fascinated that he falls like a sparrow into the enchanter's throat.
How much have young men to fear from their passions! They carry

with them a magazine that a mere spark may explode. Be on your guard, for if not subdued in youth, they may be never tamed. When the boat approaches the cataract, the pilot regrets in vain that he did not shun the current which leads to the whirlpool. The passions in youth are like race horses at a Venitian carnival. When they see the course, they break away from the grooms, dash over the ropes, and dart onward. They are like the horses of the Sun, which when driven by a Phaeton, set the world on fire. They are like the Mississippi river, which when the levee is broken down, lays waste and inundates the surrounding country.

"Is the young man safe?"—"Yes—" Satan says, "Why," he asks, "should you control your passions?—You only follow, in yielding to them, your animal instincts." True—but the instincts of man should follow him,—they were not given to be his masters, but his slaves. Thus the young man is in danger from himself.— He too often resembles the shark. No sooner does the shark see the bait dangling astern, than he dashes voraciously forward, nor ever stops, until the hook fastened in his entrails, makes him lash the waters with rage and agony.

Again, the majority of young men *care nothing for religion,*— whereas success in the game of life depends on its being conducted on religious principles. If you play at random, you will be beaten, because no moves not predicated on the will of God, are antagonist to those of your opponent. You play into his hands, unless you are governed by religious principles. For instance, your employer sends you to bank with a sum of money. He calls it a thousand dollars, but you find on counting it, that it amounts to more. Now how will you move? Will you rectify his mistake, or pocket the surplus on the plea of returning it at a future period? That depends on your religious principles. Satan moves you to take the money. You may call it borrowing, if you please. The ground on which

you may excuse doing wrong is of no consequence to Satan. You play
into his hands unless you do right.

A man has to decide in this way on right and wrong every step
that he takes on the road of life; young men especially. They are often
in positions of great temptation. Pretexts, excuses and apologies for
sin are never wanting, and without decision of character, and right
views, and settled convictions of duty; without the fear of God, and
a determination to do His will, they are as sure to fall, as a canoe in
the cataract of Niagara is of being dashed to pieces. "Is the young
man safe," who cares nothing for religion? You might as well ask if
a deserted ship is safe amid the floes and icebergs of the Arctic
Ocean. Imagine a madman steering a ship. He would not hold
her head the same way for five minutes. Governed by the whims,
and caprices of his disordered brain, he would keep her veering
about without any settled end or object, on the waters. Would that
ship be safe?—But what better than a madman is he who navi-
gates the sea of life without religion? Does he steer steadily for
the only haven where the immortal soul can find peace, and security at last? Is not his course decided by impulse, interest, con-
venience, or example? If a Roman Emperor, when he had done
nothing useful in twenty-four hours, cried out "I have lost a day,"
the man who has no aim in a right direction, may exclaim on a
death-bed, "I have lost a life—I have accomplished nothing worthy
of my existence." I do not hesitate to say that not one young
man in a hundred, will be found to make his moves on the Chess
Board of life, with a view to the final issue of the game. And
what is this but indifference to religion? You may say, perhaps,
that you respect religion; that you are not immoral; that occa-
sionally you go to church, read the bible, and say your prayers.
All this may be very true. There are different degrees of indiffe-

B

rence to religion. But do you evince that you care for religion by trying to promote its interests,—by devoting time, influence, means, and exertion to its cause;—by lending to it the vigour, and enterprize, which give such an impetus to trade, commerce, and the social projects of the day?—Do you lend a hand to the progress of truth and goodness, by aiding the reforms which the growth of vice, and increase of crime demand? Are you the willing instruments of the minister of Christ to carry out his plans of usefulness? Are you his hearers, and his helpers? Such is the importance of religion, that you cannot be acquitted of slighting it, merely because you take off your hat to it in the street, in the church, or even in your own privacy. It is a great, solemn, and and awful business, and not heartily to engage in it is indifference. It proves a man to have no such interest in religion as its importance demands. Shall I mention, in proof of the indifference of young men to religion, their aversion to religious books, religious conversation, and religious company?—Shall I mention their frequent levity of conduct in the house of God, and their reluctance to attend its solemn services? I would rather point to their total disregard of religion, as a standard of right and wrong? as the arbiter of the company they should keep, the pleasures they should indulge in, the books they should read, the places they should frequent, the habits they should form, the line of conduct they should pursue. Satan is foiled when he tempts a young man who is resolved that from his life, as from an altar of incense, there shall ascend perpetually to God the perfume of useful, virtuous and holy actions.— He is prompted at once by his religious principles to repel temptation. But, when Satan attacks one, over whom religious considerations have no power, who if he defend himself at all, does so only with earthly weapons, he is sure, sooner or later, to gain the victory. Young men whose only ambition in life is to become rich; or who care most for dress, show, pleasure, or admiration, Satan has a thousand lures for their destruction,—the wine cup, the card table, the theatre, the dance, the billiard room, the race course, with the rest of the appalling catalogue. His baits are ever at hand; and among them he is sure to find one, irresistibly attractive to young men who care nothing for religion. "Is the young man safe?"

Again, young men in general are *wise in their own conceit.*— They "think more highly of themselves than they ought to think." Many a good father can say " my son would have his own way; he was ruined by despising counsel and hating reproof. He thought he knew better what was for his good than myself." That is just the sort of young man the devil likes to meet with, one who is resolved to have his own way; for that is precisely the way wherein Satan would have him to go. It is the way to ruin; it is the way to hell, and a young man determined to travel that way, saves Satan a world of trouble. Why does Solomon say that there is more hope of a fool, than of a man wise in his own conceit; because such a man will take no advice. Advise him to take the ·Bible for his guide, and he is offended. "How humiliating" he says, " to take it for granted that every thing in the Bible is true: what becomes in that case of my independence, and freedom of thought?" Satan applauds such sentiments. He says "You are right; it is perfectly absurd to expect a man of genius, like you, to submit to its authority:" and then he suggests to the young man opinions as more worthy of his superior intellect. Many a rationalist, many a transcendentalist, many a sceptic, many an infidel, has Satan made by throwing books and men in their way to teach them opinions more flattering to intellectual pride than the gospel of Christ.— Thought in this country is free as air. Every child thinks itself entitled to an opinion. This is all very well, if we are open to conviction. But thousands of young men regard an acknowledgment that they are wrong, as tantamount to the surrender of their right to think for themselves. They oppose truth, because they will not allow they are in error. They make no enquiries, but if they were ever so much convinced, their vanity would keep them from confessing it. " Is the young man safe ?"

3. And now I am to conclude by reversing the picture. I am to show on what the young man's safety depends. His danger is evident, but on certain conditions his success is sure. In stating these, I shall be brief as possible.

First of all, *you must be Satan's enemy.* Your heart must be full of hostility to Satan. This is no sham-fight for the display of skill, but a hand to hand struggle for life, or death. If all the animosity is on Satan's side, your blows will be powerless compared with his. I remember on coming down from the pulpit one day in New York, being accosted by a young man, a perfect stranger, with the words " Do tell me, sir, how I may resist temptation." So much was he the slave of Satan that he felt degraded. He had made a thousand abortive and bootless attempts to refuse to give way to the devil, and he was frightened. With the look of one unable to withstand that power which was dragging him into deeper depths of sin, he affectingly enquired "Do tell me how I may resist temptation."—I said to him " Young man! your feeble resistance of temptation is owing to there being no enmity in your heart to the Tempter. Why do you ask me that question? Is it not because by yielding to his temptations you are disgraced? If without injury to your health, character, and position, you could persist in your present course, would you do otherwise? It is only because it is inconvenient to yield to him, that you would oppose Satan. No wonder that your opposition has been so feeble and ineffectual.— Unless God puts a burning hatred in your heart to Satan, you will never say to him when he approaches you with the dice, or wine cup —you will never indignantly say to him, "Get thee behind me, Satan"—You will never flee from him as did Joseph, when he besets you with solicitations to vice. You will never hold up your hands with horror, and cry out "How can I do this great wickedness and sin against God?" What I said to him, I say to all. To be safe, a young man must hate the Adversary of his soul.

Again, *he must be thoroughly alive to the tremendous issues of the conflict.* No man will contend with Satan to any purpose, who does not feel that he fights for something worth fighting for. See how he runs whom the Indians permit, if he can, to escape from their tomahawks! He literally flies from his pursuers. The value of life lends him nerve, speed, vigour, and endurance. So it is in the contest with Satan. The strength and ardour of our resistance will be proportioned to the value we set upon the soul. If we think of it only as a word of four letters, we shall make no exertions for its safety; but if we feel that to lose the soul, although we gained the whole world beside, would be to lose every thing, the priceless value of the soul will make us tax our energies to the utmost for its salvation. May I not appeal to young men present conscious by what stirs within them—by what they feel if they cannot see, that they have a soul—whether they are not living without concern for its safety?—whether they do not practically ignore its existence, and live as though they were made of nothing but flesh and blood! Well, to be safe, that insensibility must be removed. To rouse men from that insensibility, is the primary object of the Gospel. It is as fatal to the soul as sleep on the snows of an Arctic winter is to the body.

Again, your safety requires that you should be awakened not only to the value of the soul, but *to its guilt and danger.* So long as his victims are unconcerned upon these subjects, Satan feels secure of them. Hence he takes care not to alarm their fears. He diverts them with an infinite variety of pleasures and occupations, to deter them, if possible, from being affected by any religious influences that may be brought to bear on them, such as the ministrations of the sanctuary, the exhortations of friends, the visitations of Providence, or the Holy Scriptures, if they chance to open them.

This spell must be broken, or like an ox going to the slaughter, the young man will quietly go with the devil to his shambles.— This spell must be broken, because else, you will never seek the forgiveness which would deliver you out of his hands. Like the men in the days of Noah, who went on feasting, and drinking, and dancing, till the flood came and destroyed them all, you will persist in sin until you are drowned in the perdition of ungodly men, without the voice which some day will wake the dead in their graves, rouses you to a sense of your peril, and makes you ask with the eagerness of the Philippian gaoler, "What must I do to be saved?"

Lastly, your convictions of sin must lead you to Christ. If they fall short of this, they fall short of everything. What though they lead you in many respects to become altered men? Reformation is not conversion. Even a sinless life for the future, could not atone for a guilty life previously. Many a young man has compunctions because of its folly, and perhaps settles down into a sober, staid father and citizen, but if his youthful sins are still unblotted from God's book, he is still liable to their punishment. You must have your sins washed away in the blood of Christ. Having no righteousness of your own to plead for salvation, you must be clothed with the spotless robes of Christ's righteousness. Then you will be safe. Satan may accuse you of living whilst you were unconverted, after the devices and desires of your own heart, but Justice will say —"True, but I had satisfaction for that. Christ bore in his place the punishment of his sins, and I have no claim upon him." You will be safe from temptation, because you will hate the Tempter, hate sin, and love holiness. Thus you will "overcome the Wicked One." You will be safe in life, in death, in Judgment, and in Eternity.

THE BREAKER.

The Breaker is come up before them: they have broken **up**
and have passed through the gate and are gone out by it,
and their King shall pass before them, and the Lord on
the head of them.

Micah 2: 13.

THIS passage is variously interpreted; it seems to me, however,
very expressive of what our Joshua does for his spiritual Israel,
in order to lead them to the promised land. The name "Breaker"
suits him well, for it means what we call a Pioneer, that is, a soldier
who clears the way before an army on the march; or, if you please,
a shepherd, who removes obstacles to the advance of his flock.—
In either sense it applies to Christ, who is both the Captain of our
salvation, and the Shepherd of his people. The latter part of the
text too, which describes the army following their Leader, agrees
perfectly with what Christ says about the Church, that "he goeth
before them and the sheep follow him, for they know his voice;"
so that from this passage we may notice first, Christ opening the
way to heaven for his people; and secondly, his people following
him.

I. — *Christ* OPENING THE WAY.—The text says that "the
Breaker went up before them;" so that it was by employing *force.*
There were so many obstacles in the way of our getting there, and
such serious ones, that they could not be removed by gentle means.
Was it an easy thing, in the first place, for him *to get to us,* my
brethren? He had to employ force for that, because he had to

stoop to conquer. There he sat on his throne in heaven, with a crown of gold upon his head, and the rod of empire in his hand; and here we were crawling in the dust of the earth dishonoured, disgraced, and degraded. There he was, encircled by angels who kneeled before him, and worshipped him; who sang Te Deums in his praise, and cast their crowns at his feet; and here we were, "wretched, and miserable, and poor, and blind, and naked."— There he was, peerlessly happy in heaven, and here we were, shut up in gaol sentenced to die, and only awaiting the fatal hour. Ah! Brethren, he could not get to us without a struggle; without breaking from all that happiness, without surrendering all those honours, nay, without putting himself in our room, and becoming by imputation liable to our punishment. He had to lay aside his diadem, and his jewels, and his robes of state. He had to vacate his throne, and to forsake his glory, and to put on just such a garment as we wear, except that it was spotless and undefiled. I have read of kings, who like Charles V., gave up their thrones to escape from toil, and to avoid the bustle and trouble of the world; but when Jesus went away from heaven, it was to plunge into a sea of troubles. He left it only because we could not get there otherwise, and do you think that it cost him nothing—that he could exchange heaven for earth without a sigh? It may be a weakness, but we always shed tears on leaving home; we cannot leave the friends and protectors of our youth without a pang, and yet our sympathies compared with those of Christ are cold. Ah! Brethren, we think too little of what it cost Christ to get to us! He said to his Father, give me manhood, that I may feel as men feel; give me a human heart, that I may know the meaning of a heavy heart, an aching heart, a broken heart; give me a human body, that I may be able to bleed, to suffer, and to die: and being thus equipped he tore himself from home, broke through troops of angels who

clung about his feet, passed the golden gates, and descended on the
the wings of mercy to our guilty world. If there was ever grief in
heaven, my Brethren, it must have been on that day when Jesus
left it to come to us.

> With drooping wings the blessed Angels throng
> Around the throne; no more unite in song;
> Their harps untuned, no more they raise
> Transporting anthems and seraphic lays.
> Amazed they stand, or in low whispers tell,
> How Adam by the artful Tempter fell.
> How all his race, their Sire's rebellion share ;
> Unaided, all, its penalty must bear.
> Next, turning them to where enthroned in state,
> Reclining on his Father's bosom, sate
> The Word. This day, they add, removed to earth,
> Our Lord, by pity urged, has human birth.
> The hour is just at hand, when hence departs
> Our chiefest joy, the monarch of our hearts.
> As thus the Angels spake, the only Son
> Standing before the throne took off his crown:
> Now, He said, dear Father, hence I go
> To dwell as man, with sinful men below.
> Then off his royal mantle he did lay,
> And said, henceforth my robe will be of clay,
> And then his jewels he removed ; so bright
> That Angels' eyes are dazzled by the sight:
> Oh Father! he exclaimed, these gems retain
> Until to Heaven I return again.
> To win the crown, my Church must bear the Cross
> Be mine to show them how to gain by loss.

Again, Brethren, Jesus opened the way to heaven for his people
by *breaking the strength of sin.* That was the greatest obstacle he
had to remove. Sin is our accuser : take it away, and there is no
one to inform against us at the bar of God. All other hindrances
to our being saved, vanish like smoke when this is gone. I fear
nothing from death, I fear nothing from the grave, I fear nothing
from man, I fear nothing from heaven, I fear nothing from hell,
if I am free from sin. All that makes me tremble is sin. Why?
Because "Sin is the transgression of God's law." I would not

fear even sin were there no law, for "where there is no law there
is no transgression." This is what makes sin strong. "The strength
of sin is the law." It makes sin a punishable offence, my Brethren,
so that unless I am pardoned, it can lay hands on me, and carry me
away to prison. We say of a man in prison that his crimes brought
him there; but what gave them power to do so except the Law?
They got their strength to cast him into prison from their being
violations of the law of man, and so doth sin derive all its strength
to cast us into the prison of hell, from its being the transgression of
the law of God. Now Christ did not break the strength of sin,
by getting the law against it repealed. Men sometimes get rid of
the penalty of a law, by blotting out of the Statute Book the law
itself; but Christ broke the strength of sin, by obeying the law, and
by paying to the very uttermost all its claims. He met Sin carrying us away, as it were, to death, and He said unto him, Where
art thou going with these prisoners?—What offence have they committed?—On this Sin drew his sword, as though fearing an attempt
at rescue, and cried out, These are criminals condemned to die;
stand not in the way of the law : and at the same time, one stepped
up sword in hand, and sternly asked who hindered the Officer in
the discharge of duty. Sir, said Jesus, I have a pardon from the
King for these offenders, and with that he handed him a parchment
with the seal and sign manual of God upon it. Then the Officer,
who was no other than the Law himself, perused it, and pored over
it, and scrutinized every word of it; and he said unto Jesus, This
grants a pardon only on condition that you suffer in their stead.
I am willing to do it, said Jesus; and directly he said this, all the
prisoners looked on him and wept bitterly. Art thou willing, said
the Law, to pay all their debts, both of punishment and obedience?
Wilt thou give me full satisfaction for their past sins, and a perfect
righteousness in their stead, for the time to come? and he answered

and said unto him, I will. Then let these go their way, said the Officer, for they are "no more under the law, but under grace."— Then they "set at liberty them that were bound," and Sin leaving them, walked by the side of their Surety until the time should come for Him to redeem his promise. And did He not keep his word, my Brethren! Was he not cancelling the debt of obedience which his people owed to God's law every instant of his life! See him setting even children an example of filial love and subjection; see him teaching young men how to repel temptation, when the Devil assailed him in the desert; see him by his piety, benevolence, meekness, self-denial, and submission to God, fulfilling in our stead perfectly, to the full, and in every respect from his cradle to his grave, the spirit and the letter of the Decalogue. There was not a flaw in his life, nor a blemish in his heart, nor a taint in his thoughts; and when he had done all this, he went to Mount Calvary to redeem his bond. I see him on his way there—in the garden. Well is he called "the man of sorrows." Who ever saw a man of thirty-three with a face so seamed with care, and so marred by grief? Look at the agony in his features—listen to his groans— mark how the big tears roll down his cheeks, and how the bloody sweat mingling with them, drops upon the ground!—These were part of the expiation he engaged to make.—But see; armed men enter the enclosure with torches in their hands. Who is at their head? Surely it cannot be Judas! Ah! the audacious traitor! see, he cries, "Hail Master;" and betrays him with a kiss.

Again we are in the Prætorium, the barracks of the Roman soldiers. I see him in the midst of them like a lamb in the midst of wolves. Thou art a king, art thou? says one of them. Yes—they are deriding him—they are twining and twisting sharp thorns about his head, and calling it his crown. They put a purple robe on him, and a mock sceptre in his hand, and pretend to pay him homage.

They bind him to a pillar—See how they tear his back with whips until it streams with blood. Is there no remedy in heaven or earth for such injustice! Ye murderers of the Innocent, stop! if ye be men, stop your cruelties! This too was part of our debt which he engaged to pay. Once more, I see him again at the head of a great crowd, issuing from the gates of Jerusalem.— He walks slowly, for he is weak from loss of blood, and they have loaded his wounded back with the burden of his cross. It is too much for him to bear— he stops — and they compel Simon to carry part of it. Blessed Jesus! thus are we taught that to share thy glory, we must share thy sufferings; may we be compelled by thy amazing grace, and made willing by thy Almighty power to follow Thee whithersoever thou goest! But how shall I go on to tell the open shame they put him to? There is Sin, who has not left him a moment, driving the nails into his hands and feet, and there is the Law, like another Shylock, exacting from him the uttermost fraction of his claim, not abating a pang, a groan, or a sigh. He stands by the cross from the time it is lifted up, until the cry, "It is finished" bursts from the lips of the Crucified. Then, and not before, his grim features relax their sternness. He tears the bond he held against Jesus into tatters; and exclaiming, thou hast magnified me and made me honourable, he casts them to the winds forever. Thus Brethren, did Christ " open the kingdom of heaven to all believers," not by remitting, but by himself bearing their punishment. Though a lawful, it was a violent way of getting them there. It reminds me of the triumphant entry of a conqueror at the ancient games. He was not admitted by the gate of the city, but by a breach in the walls. The gate of merit was closed against the Sinner, and Christ by the merits of his obedience and death, has made an open- ing whereby, as a Conquering Hero, He can pass into heaven with all his people as his lawful captives. "The Breaker is come up before them; they have broken up and have passed through the gate and are gone out by it, and their King shall pass before them, and the Lord on the head of them."

Again, Christ unclosed the way to Heaven for his people, by *breaking open the tomb.* Had not Christ risen, my Brethren, what warrant would the Angel who keeps the gate of Heaven, have had for opening it to a child of Adam? Would you plead that he died for your sins? Ah! but, the Angel might say, where is the proof that his death was "a full, perfect, and sufficient sacrifice?" Where is the evidence that God is satisfied with it?—Would you plead for admission upon his merits? Then the Angel might ask, has God acknowledged their efficacy? Has he not left him in the arms of death? Is not death the wages of Sin?—How can I admit you as righteous on his account, when as yet by his remaining in the tomb his own righteousness seems questionable? Would you plead *again* that he died for your sins," then would the Angel rejoin, but he has not "risen for your justification." Before justifying others he must himself be justified. My dear Brethren, there would be no gainsaying these arguments, for, as the Apostle says, "If Christ be not raised your faith is vain, ye are yet in your sins." If I owe ten thousand dollars and you engage to pay the debt— very well—but mark you, until you actually do pay it, and get a release for me from my creditors, I am responsible nevertheless. So here, the resurrection of Christ was the receipt of God, a receipt in full for all that we owed for heaven and deserved for hell. It was the declaration of that very innocence by the imputation of which we are made out to be innocent. Unless the receipt had been given, and the declaration made, Brethren, we could never go to heaven. "But now is Christ risen," says the Apostle. "The Breaker has come up." As Sampson snapped the strong ropes of the Philistines like tow, and bore away the gates of Gaza, as if

they were feathers, so did Christ by his mighty strength and irresistible power break away from the grip of death, and the confines
of the tomb. Wonderful! do you say?—Not at all. It would be
wonderful if the dead body of a sinner should rise of itself, but
Christ was not a sinner. He only went down to the grave as the
surety of Sinners. Having done that it was enough, and death
having no claim upon him personally, could not retain him in his
bonds. "It was impossible that he should be holden of them."
We have seen Egyptian mummies that death has kept fast hold of
for a thousand years. Such is the strength which death acquires
over sinners, that for thousands of years he keeps them in prison.
Whereas Christ being without sin escaped from him on the third
day. Look at that cloud over the sun; it is black as ink, and for
an instant or two may intercept his rays, but wait a moment and
see if it do not break through and be all the more glorious for its
brief eclipse; so Christ, the Sun of Righteousness emerged by virtue of his own power, from the pitchy darkness of the grave. They
wound him in grave-clothes, they covered his face with a napkin,
they laid him in a rocky crypt, they closed up his tomb with an
enormous stone, they sealed it, they set a watch on it, but as our
Hymn says—

> "Vain the stone, the watch, the seal,
> Christ has burst the gates of hell;
> Death in vain forbids him rise,
> Christ has opened paradise."

"The Breaker has come up before them, they have broken up
and have passed through the gate and are gone out by it; and
the King shall pass before them, and the Lord on the head of
them."

Again, Christ opened the way to heaven for his people by *going
there himself.* They go there only as his followers, and except in

his train as their forerunner and representative, they could not go there at all. The ascension of Christ to heaven therefore, secured for his people a right to ascend there too. What else did he mean by saying to his disciples, "I go to prepare a place for you," but that there would be no place for them, unless he preceded them to his Father's house? It is true that there are many mansions in heaven; so there are many mansions on earth, but what are we the better of that who are no householders? Take possession for me of one of those mansions, reserve it for me, and have it all ready for me to go into on my arrival, and then it is a great thing for me to know that there are many mansions in heaven. I am glad of it. I shall have a home to go to. The object of Christ's ascension was to provide such a home. Ah, Brethren, how few there be who think of heaven as a home! how few there be who say about it as they do when travelling, of their earthly abode, I am tired of journeying, there is no place like home. Men speak often of their comfortable homes, their pleasant homes; but how seldom do we hear them talking of their heavenly homes! Alas, that so many should have no prospect before them beyond the grave! They have a snug house by the sea-side, or a splendid mansion in town, or a fine farm in the country; but they have no place provided for them in heaven. But of the Christian it can be said, that he has "a house not made with hands, eternal in the heavens," for Christ has gone there before to provide it for him. He can say, I am not going to die on a venture; death will not cast me ashore, and land me a total stranger in the eternal world. I am an adopted citizen of heaven, I own a house there, I have laid up treasure there, and when I arrive there all the inhabitants will bid me welcome. Christian! thy Lord hath thus opened heaven for thee that thou mightest enjoy the comfort of seeing it before getting there. By going there himself he has placed it full in your view. Look through the perspective glass that Bunyan speaks of, and you catch a sight of the gates, and of the glory of the city. Mind Christian, that was to cheer you, to increase your earnestness, and to enable you to set little store by the present world.

> " We've no abiding city here;
> Then let us live as pilgrims do,
> Let not the world our rest appear,
> But let us haste from all below."

Observe again that unless Christ had gone up to heaven, *the Holy Spirit would not have come down from Heaven.* "If I go not away, the Comforter will not come unto you," said Christ, and without the sanctifying influences of the Holy Ghost, none of us could enter Heaven. What, may I not be admitted there if Christ has prepared a place for me? No, is the reply, not unless you are prepared for the place. May I not enter in the robe of his righteousness? the reply is, that Christ does not disguise sinners with that robe, and steal them under cover of it into Heaven. "Whom he justifies, them he also sanctifies." "Without holiness, no man shall see the Lord." If he casts the robe of his righteousness over your shoulders, he breathes the spirit of his holiness into your heart. When Mantua was assailed by the French, the Austrians attempted to relieve the garrison disguised in white cloaks to resemble the French Hussars; but the deceit, owing to some inconsistency of dress was detected, and the drums beat, and the barricades shut in an instant. Dost thou think, Sinner, to enter Heaven by a stratagem like that? To cover a sinner's heart with a saint's dress, and so find admission? Why the angels would see through you in an instant; they would know you were an enemy in disguise, and the gates would turn instinctively on their hinges to bar you out.—

Never, though your life were a Lent, and your abode a hermitage; never, though you wasted your flesh with fasting, and practised all the austerities of the sternest anchorite, can you obtain admission into heaven, except you have been born again, and so by the power of the Holy Ghost have been " made meet for the inheritance of the Saints in Light." Then, I repeat, that as the Holy Ghost would not have descended from heaven, if Christ had not ascended there, by doing so, he has given us a powerful friend in heaven; one who will use all his influence there in our behalf, one who has gone there as our high priest, so that "if any man sin, we have an advocate with the Father, even Jesus Christ the Righteous." Did you ever notice, Brethren, that when Christ ascended to heaven, it is said by St. Luke that he "led his disciples as far as Bethany?" It seems like the eagle, the bird of the sun, leading out its brood, and teaching them to soar by soaring himself to heaven before their eyes. Oh may we follow in heart, where he ascended in body; "setting our affections on things in heaven, not on things on the earth." Gazing like the unfledged eaglet upward to our native skies, so that at length, we too may follow our ascended Lord, and our death may be spoken of only as the upspringing of the lark from its lowly nest.

> "The cheerful lark, mounting from early bed
> With sweet salutes awakes the drowsy light,
> The earth she left, and up to heaven is fled.
> There chants her Maker's praises out of sight."

II.—I have little time left to speak of how the people of Christ follow him to heaven, and I must content myself with the single remark that they must first of all *be made willing to follow him.* They follow him willingly, patiently, faithfully, hopefully and triumphantly. They follow him willingly at their conversion, patiently in their trials, faithfully in their duties, hopefully in their death, and triumphantly in their ascension; but I must confine myself to the grave fact, that without they are made willing, they will not follow him at all. There is naturally a deadness in our hearts to the whole subject of religion. It is not one which we like to talk about or think upon. Who is there that has not secretly felt and acknowledged that by nature he is not willing to follow Christ? Many, I believe, have acknowledged it upon their knees to God. They have said, my heart is like stone, as cold, as hard, and as unfeeling, O God! what will become of me when I die? Yes brethren, the great obstacle to our following Christ, lies in our hearts. Many are willing to go to church for Christ, and to give their money for Christ, and to read their Bible for Christ, and to do many other things for him; but there is one thing which they will not do, and without which, though they "gave all their goods to feed the poor, and their bodies to be burned," they will fall short of heaven; and that is, they will not give their hearts to Christ. *That* we must be made willing to do, my Brethren. Every man has a heart to give to Christ, if he have nothing else. But if you have everything else, he will accept of nothing unless you give him *that*. Mark again— Christ does not tell us to follow him as a good man, a moral man, an amiable man, a benevolent man; He bids you follow him as the Saviour of sinners, so that your doing so depends on your feeling yourself to be a sinner. If you feel yourself to be a sinner, then you will follow him, because he came into the world to save sinners. And as to the way in which we are made willing, or what is the same thing, convinced of our need of Jesus, it is by the constraining power of Christ himself. By his Spirit he will convince you of sin, bring you within the attraction of his cross, and then, my dear hearer, you will love him for laying down his life for you; then you will be impelled by gratitude, by affection, by a sense of duty and danger to follow him, and you will say what I trust is the language of all here :

> "Jesus, I my cross have taken,
>   All to leave and follow thee;
> All things else for thee forsaken,
>   Thou from hence my all shall be."

FOR EVER AND EVER.

"For ever and ever."

You may not think much of this text because it is only a phrase; but for all that it has a solemn sound, and no sentence is more expressive than some sounds are. The sound of the airs which we were used to in childhood for instance; or, after being absent for years from home, the sound of the church bells in our native place. It will touch the heart, and bring tears into the eyes when nothing else will. These are suggestive sounds, and so is " for ever and ever," a suggestive sound.

I. —*First, it reminds us of the past, and raises the spectres of departed things.*

1. Look at that troop of little ones. It is hard to believe that we were ever like that playful child, that light hearted boy. I look on them, and see in their sunny faces, no signs of care, or sorrow, or suffering. I see them clap their little hands at a rainbow, shout with joy at a sparrow, and to go into raptures with a rose. I see them saying their prayers, or repeating with reverence their evening hymns. Is it possible that we ever resembled them, that we were ever as artless, as simple, and as natural as they are: that we were once like that little "child?"

"Tossing its merry head of ringlets wild?"

Yes—and as we look on that troop of little ones, they turn to us all and say, " We are gone ' for ever and ever.' "

2. Look again at that figure, seated on a rock, with a dark mantle on his shoulders. He has been sitting there, my friends, ever since we were born, and there he will sit until we draw our last breath, and go to render our account to God. He has an ink-horn in one hand, and a pen in the other, with which he records on a scroll our misspent hours. His name is Time. See how his head bends over the scroll, and his hand writes on it without a pause, nor doth he ever raise his voice until the year's end, when in sepulchral tones he exclaims as the clock strikes twelve, "For ever and ever!"—See how he frowns, and shakes his hoary head when you ask him to blot out a page, or even to run his pen through a line of that faithful record. Ah! Brethren, which of us has not cause to sigh when he thinks of the past! One of the Martyrs, it is said, on first going into court was very talkative, until a noise behind the hangings, like that of some one taking notes, put a stop to it. Oh! why were we not on our guard against sin, when we knew that Time with his note book was behind the curtain! We have forgotten that a reporter was present who omits nothing, and extenuates nothing, and alters nothing; who, if we were to sue with tears of blood for an erasure, would say as Pilate did to the Jews, "Quod scripsi, scripsi," What I have written, I have written. It will go hard with us, Brethren, if this witness appear against us at the bar of God. "What need is there," He will say, "of further evidence? These pages contain all his thoughts, words, and deeds from his cradle to his grave. Take him away, ye Angels,—cast him into outer darkness; there shall be weeping, and wailing, and gnashing of teeth." Oh, Sinner! never let that record of Time be brought against thee at the day of Judgment! Thou canst not steal it, nor tear it, nor cut a leaf out of it, nor consume it. If thou were to cast it into hell fire, it would burn like asbestos, without being singed. Thou canst only sprinkle the blood of Christ upon it; without that, it will confront thee "for ever and ever."

It is the impossibility of revoking the past that makes these words solemn. If we could recall time and live over again our misspent years, we might make better use of them and have less to answer for. No man ever wished to live over again, for any other end than to live better. "Had I but one year more," said a dying scholar, "it should be spent in studying David's Psalms, and Paul's Epistles."—"And must I then die," said one, "Will not all my riches save me. I could purchase the kingdom if that would prolong my life."—Ah! there be many who have spent all their time in making money, who would give at last all the money they have made for an hour of time. There be many who, for a day to transact their business with heaven, would sign a cheque for all the profits they have made by their business on earth. This shows the value of time. "Throw *years* away!—Throw empires and be *blameless; Moments* seize; *Heaven's* on their wing: a moment we may wish when *worlds* want wealth to *buy*."

3. "For ever and ever." These words remind us again of the *opportunities* we have lost. The poet says, that "there is a tide in the affairs of men which taken at the flood leads on to fortune," but how many miss the tide! You often hear people say that they have lost a chance; that they could have bought a lot for hundreds, which is now worth thousands; they had the chance, but they let it slip. Reason in the same way about higher things, and who has not lost a thousand chances! Let me just remind you of some of them. Young man, you have lost a chance. You were better off than nine-tenths of your generation in having *pious parents*. That was their Bible, will you lend it me a moment. See how often tears were in their eyes when they read this book. Look how it has been pored over, and thumbed, and marked, and folded. "My son," they used to say, "read your Bible, search the Scriptures." You

paid no regard to it, but many a time have they begged you even
with tears to seek the Lord, to seek him with your whole heart.
Here is your Mother's name. Ah! she taught you the first prayer
you ever lisped, and the first hymn you ever sung, and the first
lessons from the sacred volume you ever learned. Don't you remember how sad she looked when you had done wrong? Cannot you
see her now in that little room, where you have often knelt by
her side? There she sits in the old arm-chair giving you advice, or
kneeling pours out her heart for you at a throne of grace. Are
not your worst faults, and habits, and tempers the very ones
against which she gave you warning? Have not many errors of
your life been owing to your neglect of the—"don't do that, my
child; leave that alone; have nothing to say to him;" of a pious
mother? She tried to nip sin in the bud, so that being repressed
in youth, it might give you less trouble to keep it under in after
life. Cumming says, that when hunting in Africa, he dragged a
serpent fifteen feet long out of his den by main force; but the serpent sin, cannot be dislodged in that way; you must starve it to
prevent its growing to be fifteen feet long, else you will have a
nest of such monstrous serpents in your bosom, that it will be hard
to deny them any thing. Your mother's object in opposing your
will and thwarting your wishes; her aim in all the restraints, and
checks, and curbs she put upon you, was to hinder the growth of
inbred sin; and now that you have reached manhood without profiting by her counsel; now that she can neither plead with you,
nor pray for you any more; now that the hand which used to press
yours so kindly is cold, and you have lost the benefit of the good
example and timely warnings of pious parents, you have lost chances
of salvation more precious than the gold of Ophir. Here is their
Bible. If you read it and pray over it, their prayers in your behalf
may yet be answered, but still you have lost golden opportunities;

you made light of them; you let them slip; and they are gone " for ever and ever."

II.—*But I would have you to notice in the next place, that these words are not applicable to any thing temporal.* You can find nothing on earth that is "for ever and ever;" although to see men running to and fro as they do now in quest of wealth, you might think differently. You might suppose that the objects of human pursuit were eternal, when you see how hard men toil for them, but it is not so; nothing lasts long here. We learn this from what can no longer be found upon the earth, although at one time thought imperishable;—from the famous cities of which nothing is left to us but the name; from the treasures that have been scattered to the winds, and from the great works of antiquity which have left no trace behind. We learn it from the ruins of empires, from the faded glory of Babylon, and Persia, and Greece, and Rome, and from the myriads who have disappeared from this mortal scene; above all we learn it from what is going on before our eyes; for could we look down upon all the present generation at a glance, as Xerxes looked upon his countless host, we might weep as he did, at the thought that fifty years hence not one of them will be alive. Let me add too, that the same truth is written in the book of Nature; in the fitful sky that is serene one minute, and stormy the next; in the treacherous deep, that sleeps to-day and is rough to-morrow; in the veering winds, in the shifting seasons, in the scudding clouds, in the ebbing tides, and in the falling leaves. Do you suppose that the analogy between what we see in nature, and what we are ourselves is owing to chance? Do you suppose that the abode of mortals tallies by accident with their unhappy state? I tell you that God made nature to be a book of types, that we might read even in the descending sun, and in the falling leaves, and in the shooting stars, and in the fading flowers, that nothing on earth lasts forever.—

Sinner! thou wouldst stay here; thou askest no better heaven than what this world can furnish: Thou art saying to thy soul—"Soul, thou hast much goods laid up for many years, take thine ease, eat, drink, and be merry;" but for all that the day is at hand when thy soul will be required of thee. In place then, of saying what shall I do to pass away time? thou oughtest to say, what shall I do when time is past? Think of Eternity;—if you had Eternity in your thoughts, you would never consent for the repose of an hour on a bed of roses here, to lie " for ever and ever" on a bed of thorns hereafter. I remember reading of a young man who on entering a theatre, heard a voice saying unto him in solemn tones, " *that is the way down to the pit*," and so shocked was he that it made him serious for the rest of his life. Oh! Sinner, hear Eternity saying the same thing to thee, and perhaps it may produce the like effect. That is the way, the very way thou art following—that is the way down to the pit.

> " Lord, open Sinners' eyes
>   Their awful state to see;
> And make them ere the storm arise
>   To thee for safety flee."

III.—But I come now to inquire, in the third place, *what it is that corresponds with the words "for ever and ever."*

1. *God* is " for ever and ever." This is plain from the fact of His being God, for it is inconsistent with the idea of God, that He is not eternal. As the cause of all things, He must be Himself uncaused. He is not a self-made God, nor a God made by another, nor the effect of chance, so that except He is eternal it is inconceivable how He can be God at all. This is so plain even to infidels, that the Turks cry out every day from their mosques, " God always was, and always will be," and the heathen of old denoted the same thing by a symbol. They made a circle the emblem of God;

they made their temples circular, and the Pythagoreans worshipped
God turning round and round, because they regarded Him as
without beginning or end, as enclosing all things, but enclosed by
nothing; like a circle whose "centre is everywhere, and circumfe-
rence nowhere." It were strange indeed to say of God, that there
was a time when He had no existence, for a finite God were no
God at all. If you limit His duration, you limit His power, His
goodness, His truth, for he who is not infinite in every perfection
is so in none. And yet further, we are sure that God is eternal;
for we are taught in the Scriptures, that "with Him is no varia-
bleness, neither shadow of turning." Accordingly He must have
always been the same as He is now, and He must always continue
to be the same as He is now. On this account, when Moses asked
God for His name, God gave him one that expresses what distin-
guishes Him from all creatures as being the only necessarily immu-
table and eternal Being in the Universe. The name "I AM" implies that God is always the same. Who but God could possibly
appropriate to himself such a name as this. Were Columbus living,
he might point to many a towering landmark, and say,—"Thou art
the same!—Three hundred and sixty years have made in thee no
change." Were Noah living, he might point to Ararat, and say,—
"Thou art the same as when my ark grounded on thy rocky summit." Were Adam living, he might point to the Euphrates, and
say,—"Thou art the same as when thou wateredst Eden."—The
Angels, when they look down upon the earth, can say,—"Thou art
the same as when first we saw thee projected into space;"but before
the foundations of the earth were laid—before a mortal breathed—
before an Angel shook his wings—before a planet rolled—or a sun
blazed, God was what he now is—aye, and after the earth shall
be burnt up, and the heavens shall have passed away with a
great noise, He will continue the same. His name is "I AM,"

B

because "as He was in the beginning" so He "is now and ever shall be, world without end." He is like the promontory of ages, on which "in vain the envious surges beat," whilst such creatures as we are, like drift-wood in the torrent, hurry by him to destruction. God is "for ever and ever."

Now before I pass on, what shall I put after these words for our instruction? Listen—God is "for ever and ever" *merciful*. Let us learn from that to be merciful ourselves. The world is more cruel than death. Look at that man in rags and tatters.—Oh! he is a worthless fellow, you say, he has lost friends, name, fortune, everything by intemperance. Yes, and what is worst of all, he has lost hope; and it was less his vice, than the scorn and contempt of his fellow-men, that made him desperate. The world has no mercy on these poor creatures, or many of them might be reclaimed, but the world drives them to despair by cruel, harsh, and unfeeling treatment. God Almighty is ready to forgive them, but the world cries, "Away with them, it is not fit that such wretches should live." Look at the prodigal; was not his Father glad to see him come back, although in rags and wretchedness? Did he not go out to meet him, although he had not a coin in his pocket, having spent the last cent he had in riotous living? Did he not even when he was yet a long way off, run and fall on his neck, and kiss him, and put the best robe he had on him? Let us learn, I say, from the eternal mercy of God to be ourselves merciful. I have read that a lion in the Roman amphitheatre, when one was thrown to him, who had done him a kindness, instead of tearing him to pieces, began to lick his hands. When shall we attempt to reform men by the kindness which has tamed lions? Never strike a fallen man, never spurn a man of broken fortunes, take him by the hand before he mingles the poison or sharpens the knife of the

suicide. The mercy of God is eternal, so that it is never too late
to do him good. You may lead him to Christ, you may "save a
soul from death, and hide a multitude of sins." "Blessed are the
merciful; for they shall obtain mercy."—There be some Christians
who talk of God's mercy as people who keep barometers in their
houses talk of the weather; when all goes well with them, and the
sun shines and the mercury rises, they are all smiles and full of
praises; but when the glass falls their spirits fall along with it.
Such persons need to be reminded that God's mercy is eternally
the same. Art thou in great straits? is the companion of thy life
taken away, or is the child of thy love at the point of death? Art
thou suffering in person or estate?—still remember that God hath
"not forgotten to be gracious." Remember that afflictions are but
blessings in disguise, and that "the darkest hour of the twenty-four
is that just before day-break."

> "Though waves and storms go o'er my head,
> Though strength, and health, and friends be gone,
> Though joys be withered all, and dead,
> Though every comfort be withdrawn;
> Steadfast on this my soul relies,
> Father! Thy mercy never dies."

Let me observe too that God is "for ever and ever" *rich*. The
orphan, the widow, the unfortunate, the church and all the charitable institutions of Christendom would be better off, were it remembered that God is inexhaustibly rich. Look at that Christian with
a hundred dollar bill in his hand; "Shall I give all this," he says, "to
the poor?" "Yes, quick;" "Ah! but will God make it good to me?"
Is not God for ever and ever rich then? Does not his truth endure
for ever and ever? and has he not said, "He that hath pity upon
the poor lendeth unto the Lord, and look, what he layeth out it shall
be paid him again."—There be many who will not *trust* God; they
will give you cash in a moment for what they call good paper, but

see how their faces elongate when you ask them to cash one of *God's* promissory notes.

One more thought upon this head—God's *love* is "for ever and ever." What does He say Himself about this? He says "If My children forsake My law, then will I visit their transgressions with the rod; nevertheless My lovingkindness will I not utterly take from him nor suffer My faithfulness to fail." I have known many a Christian when he stood most in need of the comfort of that promise, to have most difficulty in realizing it. There is a poor man about to die, he has been faithful in a very little, he has fallen into many a sin, and been overcome by many a temptation; the tears are running down his cheeks at the recollection of his folly. Ah! he says, "I will arise and go to my Father"—but will he receive such a sinner as I am; will He not turn such an ungrateful wretch away? Will He whom I have so often offended, welcome me home? Yes, indeed, my penitent brother, thou mayest be sure of a gracious welcome, for God "rests in his love"—"whom He loves, He loves unto the end." He loves them ".for ever and ever."

But on the other hand, the eternity of God's perfections is as awful to the Sinner, as it is encouraging to the Saint. There are ways of eluding punishment here. Human justice is not always even-handed; but how wilt thou escape, Sinner, from the incorruptible Judge, whose justice is eternally true, and whose power to punish is eternally strong?—Perhaps you say, "Oh! when it comes to the point, He will let us off, He will not be strict to mark iniquity, His threatenings are more to frighten us than anything else." Ah! but, if God's truth is "for ever and ever," He will *keep His word.* Be not deceived.

> "The vilest wretch that breathes the air
> Has now no reason to despair,"

but do not persist in a course of sin in the belief that God will break his word. " Heaven and Earth"—yon starry host that have been sparkling in the sky for ages; the sun and moon which have never failed to run their course, the earth, which with undeviating regularity has observed its seasons, these "shall pass away"—but my word," saith God Almighty, "shall not pass away."

IV.—Lastly, *and it embraces all with which we have any concern on this subject.—The Soul* is " for ever and ever." This may be proved from its *nature.* It is made to last, it is not made of perishable materials. As I judge whether you mean a build- ing to last by the materials you build it with, so I infer that the soul is immortal from its having a spiritual and immate- rial nature. Men do not expect even their granite buildings to last for ever; but there is no cause of decay in the soul, nor any external power that can wear it away. It is proof against all assaults from without, and it has no root of corruption within.— Do you imagine that *God* will kill the soul? No doubt, He could; but there is no fickleness of purpose about God. He made the soul to last, and therefore last it will " for ever and ever." And let me say again that if the soul were not eternal, men would be less *anxious* than they are *about the future.* The Sinner often says to himself as he nears the grave, " Oh God ! what will become of my soul? I must live differently, I must be resolute and give up this or that, or I shall be lost." What are all thy good intentions, Sinner? What thy broken resolves, thy fits of prayer, thy parox- ysms of piety, but the intimations of conscience that thy soul is eternal? Thou hast often gone upon thy knees, although thou didst forget the next moment all about it; thou hast often begun to read the Scriptures, although thou hast become tired in a day or two;—thou hast often, although, with no tenacity of purpose, tried to break off thy sins. Be assured that the soul knows well the tremendous stakes that are depending on the thread of life. Why when a man is truly converted to God he is literally and visibly a "new creature," the joy of the soul sparkles in his eyes, and lights up the gloomiest visage on earth.

> "Ah! who can tell the joy
>   Which reigns within the breast,
> Where heavenly dews of grace descend,
>   And Jesus is the guest!"

Does it not argue the soul to be eternal that she laughs and sings when she is secure of future blessedness; and groans and moans, and trembles whilst her destiny still vibrates betwixt heaven and hell? Sinner, thy fears, thy dark and melancholy moods, are nothing less than the forebodings of the soul, and unless thou findest refuge in Christ they will all be realized, for the soul is immortal and hell is eternal, and where the soul goes when it quits the body, there it will remain "for ever and ever."

> "Infinite years in torment must I spend,
> And never—never—never—at an end?
> Ah! must I lie in torturing despair,
> As many years as atoms in the air?
> When these are spent, as many thousand more
> As grains of sand that crowd the ebbing shore!
> When these are gone, as many to ensue
> As stems of grass on hill and dale that grew;
> When these are out, as many on the march
> As starry lamps that gild the spangled arch;
> When these expire, as many millions more
> As moments in the millions past before:—
> When all these doleful years are spent in pain,
> And multiplied by myriads again,
> Till numbers drown the thought—Could I suppose
> I *then* should terminate my wretched woes,
> This would afford some ease—but oh! I shiver
> To think upon the doleful sound—'For ever.'
> The burning gulf—where I blaspheming lie
> Is no more time—but vast Eternity."

I close with a thought as common as the air we breathe. It is this—Christ died to save the soul. That is the strongest proof of its eternity that I know of. May God impress it on every heart. "If I do not die," He said, "my church will die, 'for ever and ever,'" and so he went "like a sheep to the slaughter." "He was dumb, He opened not his mouth." He was confounded by the thought, unless I die, they will die "for ever and ever."—It was always in his mind. When his heart was wrung in the garden—When the blood started from his pores—When they exposed him naked on the cross,—At every stroke of the whip, at every blow of the hammer, at every pang that shot through his frame, he was held up by the thought, Unless I die, my people will die "for ever and ever." Ah! poor Sinner, art thou thinking how much time thou hast lost, how many opportunities thou hast let slip, what good parents thou hast made light of?—Art thou reflecting on thy sins, and saying to thyself, Life is short, death is near—my soul is immortal—"What must I do to be saved?" "Behold the Lamb of God, that taketh away the sin of the world!" Look at Him.—Cry, "Lord save or I perish;" and if thou art indeed humbled and penitent, and believing, He will give thee everlasting life, and He will raise thee up at the last day, and thou shalt live with Him "for ever and ever."

WHY WE USE A PRAYER BOOK.

<hr>

" Let all things be done decently and in order."

I Cor. 14: 40.

THE Apostle speaks here of public worship, which was conducted among the Corinthians in a disorderly manner. Every one had something to say, even the women; and every one wanted to take precedence in speaking. "How is it," says the Apostle, "when ye come together, every one of you hath a psalm, hath a doctrine, hath a tongue, hath a revelation, hath an interpretation?"—"Let all things be done decently and in order." Public worship should be performed with decorum. To prevent confusion it should be well ordered. Every thing should be done in it at the proper time, and by the proper persons, and there should be a congruity between the postures of the worshippers and the several parts of the Service. Moreover, every thing that is said in public worship should be intelligible to the meanest capacity, and express the common wants of mankind. It should be simple, reverential, and thoroughly in accordance with the Word of God. I believe that with these principles our services are in perfect keeping. How fully they comply with them I shall attempt to show in these Lectures. We think that even the use of a form of prayer contributes to order and decency in public worship, and I shall devote this evening to the answering of a question which is often put to Episcopalians; namely, why they read the prayers out of a book in place of saying what occurs to them at the time, or what previously to going to Church they have prepared? It is important that our reasons for doing this should be understood, because the practice is often condemned from ignorance of the grounds on which it is founded.

I. We do so in the first place *out of reverence and respect to God*. We run the risk of speaking unadvisedly with our lips, if we say in prayer what first occurs to us. See what absurdities people who talk without weighing their words fall into. They hurt the feelings of good men, and excite the ridicule of others. Our Prayers have precisely an opposite effect. To good men they are edifying, to bad they are a rebuke. They assist the devotion of the one, and repress the levity of the other. As the results of previous thought they are certainly more respectful than any thing we could say without reflection; and they are likely to be more effectual. One reason assigned in Scripture for our prayers being unanswered is, that " we ask amiss," and what is more likely to make us do so, than not to take time to think what we ought to ask for? This then is one reason for using a form of prayer. We think that it consists better than extempore prayer with the respect due to the Object of our worship. We think that if in conversation we measure our words, for fear of the consequences of a slip of the tongue, we should be much more careful to weigh the expressions with which we address the Almighty. Others may think differently. They are welcome to their opinion, but this is ours. The wise man says, "Keep thy foot when thou goest into the House of God," referring to our conduct in a place of worship; and it seems to us that he includes what we *say*, as well as what we do there by such a caution.

II. Another reason for our using a form of prayer is, that *it comports better with the nature of Public Worship* which requires the prayers to be such that all can unite in them. They to whom they are unsuitable are thereby excluded from public worship. So far as they are concerned the Minister might as well pray in an unknown tongue. His words might as well be above their comprehension as unfit for their use. Now to precompose such prayers as are suited to a promiscuous assemblage of people is very difficult, but to make them off hand, as the saying is, or with only a brief preparation before entering the desk, I venture to say is impossible. An extempore prayer is likely to be anything but Common prayer, or one applicable to public devotion. The speaker usually forgets that in place of being in his closet making known to God his own particular case, he is in the sanctuary representing the varied necessities of a large body of worshippers. He goes into details which do not apply to the case of other people if they do to his, or else he omits something which individuals would wish the whole congregation to unite in asking. They have a sick relative or friend perhaps, or one who has just sailed on a long and perilous voyage; or they have some secret trouble of their own, and as the prayer of a righteous man availeth much, they would like the whole church to intercede for them, but they are disappointed. The Minister says what first occurs to him, and it never occurs to him to say what they wish to hear. Nor is he to be blamed, for even. if he knew the besetting sins and necessities and trials and state of mind of every man in his congregation, he could not possibly advert to each and all of them. In public worship the petitions must be of such a general character, as to admit of each worshipper glancing at the particulars of his own case. The wife for instance whose husband is in California, cannot expect the minister a stranger to her, to pray specifically for his safe return, but when he prays God generally "to preserve all who travel by land or by water," she can under that general head pray for her husband in particular. But to do that, she ought to know beforehand what the speaker is going to say. Can you catch the sense, and adopt the wish of petition after petition, as they fall from the lips of one who prays extempore

in public? Does he not get in advance of you? Whilst you are
digesting his present request, has he not gone two or three requests
beyond? In that case, it seems to me that you do not pray at all.
You hear what he says, but as to going along with him intellectual-
ly and spiritually, it is out of the question. You are like spectators
in a Court of Justice. They listen to the eloquent address of counsel, they feel its pathos and power, and they admire its ability;
but as for themselves they are silent. Whilst the prayer is going
on, you listen, wonder, and perhaps secretly applaud the beauty of
expression, but it is the Minister who prays, not you. You cannot,
because unless you understand a petition, you cannot say amen to
it; and you do not get time to understand one petition, before the
speaker goes on to another. A book is needed, in order that Common Prayer may be going on throughout the assembly, that each
may interpret the prayers for himself as the speaker proceeds.

III. Again, Episcopalians prefer forms of prayer, because they
are *protected by them from the fluctuations and inequalities in point*
of excellence, which are inseparable from extemporaneous prayers.
Not only have men different degrees of understanding and education
and piety, but they possess in very different degrees the power of
expressing their thoughts. Some are slow, obscure, and hesitating:
it is painful to listen to them. Some are at a loss for words, and
some for ideas. Some are too low in their vocabulary, and some too
high. And besides these differences, such are the infirmities of
human nature, that you are never sure if he who leads your devotions extempore, is physically qualified for the task. The mind
sympathizes with the body, and if indisposed, the speaker's power of
performing this duty with acceptance is diminished. But when a
form is used, all these difficulties are obviated. The people are certain, whatever be the talents or capacity of the minister, whether he
be slow of speech, dull of comprehension, or in bad health, that the

excellence of the prayers will not be affected by it. Besides, you
must remember that some men are very eccentric and prejudiced
and imprudent. If any particularly exciting topic is before the
public, they are likely enough to give you a lecture upon it in devotional form. They say odd things, injudicious things, and give
vent in prayer to their peculiarities. You want protection from
prayers tinctured by these causes; else your feelings will be often
hurt, and your taste offended, and your understanding insulted.—
A form gives you that protection. It obliges the speaker to confine
himself to the book, and restrains him from indulging in his own
vagaries. Moreover, even a beautiful extempore prayer has this
drawback that when I am admiring the eloquence and sublimity
of a prayer which I never heard before, I am not attending to the
duty of prayer myself. I am doing homage rather to a fellow worm,
than to God. In an old familiar form there is no such temptation. The speaker did not compose it. I am not thinking at all
of the speaker. I am wholly occupied in pouring out my heart
to God.

IV.—Another reason for our using forms of prayer is that they
are *a means of preserving purity of doctrine in the Church.* Let
him say what he will in the pulpit, the minister is not permitted
in the prayers to depart from what is written; and the people can
easily judge, with the Prayer Book in their hands, of the difference
in doctrine between the pulpit and the reading-desk. The reading-
desk teaches the doctrine of the Church, the pulpit the doctrine of
the man, and any discrepancy between them is easily detected.—
I read in a Church paper the other day, that at the late General
Convention a presbyter "related an incident of two clergymen
coming from the North to the South, one a Congregationalist and
the other an Episcopalian. Both imbibed heretical sentiments.
In the case of the Congregationalist there was nothing to prevent

him from preaching and praying his own opinions, and the consequence was that his congregation became indoctrinated with his
heresies; whereas the Episcopalian, being compelled to conform to
the Liturgy, was obliged to leave the Church, and not one of his
hearers would go along with him." This illustrates what I mean
when I say that forms of prayer keep the doctrines of the Church
pure. They made it impossible for the heretical minister conscien-
tiously to continue within her pale, and they protected the people
from infection by his errors. In many a pulpit, owing to the want
of a prayer book, Unitarianism has supplanted Orthodoxy. The
Puritans were great foes to Episcopacy, but if those grim Christians
could leave their graves, they would be shocked to find that many
of their descendants, have fallen into errors a thousand fold more
hateful to them than the doctrines and discipline of the Church of
England. But it would surprise them most to learn that the Liturgy
of that Church, which they used to inveigh against so bitterly, has
been the means of keeping her head the right way, whilst for want
of it their own people have run ashore. I do not put the Prayer
Book on a par with the Bible—God forbid. But it contains nothing
contrary to the Bible. It is a summary of the doctrines of the
Bible, and as such it is of great worth. Episcopalians keep the
prayer book in their houses, in their parlours; they take it to
Church, they use it in their family, and by its frequent use they
are qualified to judge how far any doctrines propounded to them
are scriptural. Our Creeds and Articles and Prayers being strictly
in accordance with the Word of God, you need only try any error
in circulation by our Standards, to expose its fallacy. Owing to
the Prayer Book very few Episcopalians leave their Church. You
hear sometimes of their going over to the Church of Rome. Every
rule has its exceptions. But the numbers who have done so have
been comparatively very small. I have seen it stated that in the

last twelve years one hundred and fifty clergymen of the Church of England have so apostatized. It should be remembered, however, that there are eighteen thousand clergymen in the Church of England. You must remember that Rome makes no impression at all on our masses either in England or in the United States.— Not here certainly, for even in those Episcopal Churches where by additions to the Prayer Book they attempt to go back of the Reformation the attendance is very small. Attachment to the Prayer Book of the Reformation prevents sound Churchmen either here or in England, from countenancing usages analogous to those of the Missal and Breviary.

V. Take one more reason for our using forms. Their use is sanctioned by *Scripture* and *by the example of Christians in the earliest times.* Look at the Psalter. David wrote the Psalms to be set to Church Music. Their structure proves that they were composed for the temple worship. In the twenty-sixth chapter of Deuteronomy, and in the sixth of the book of Numbers, you will find prayer ordained by God himself, to be used in divine service by his ancient people. Besides, their descendants now who still follow the practice of their forefathers in this particular, are witnesses that both in the temple and in their synagogues the ancient Jews used forms of prayer. Let it be remembered, then, that our Saviour and his Apostles were Jews. We find them conforming to the temple worship. We find the Apostles asking our Lord to teach them " to pray as John taught his disciples." The Lord's Prayer is a form. By giving them this He justified the use of forms under the Gospel. He did not give them this prayer as the only form they should use, but he taught them to use forms by saying, "after this manner pray ye." The fact is, that you can trace in the customs of the early Christian Church, that its founders were

B

Jews. There is an analogy between the Bishop and the High Priest, between the Presbyters and inferior Priests, between the Deacons and Levites. The consecration of a Bishop, his vestments, and the vestments of Presbyters, all have their types in the Jewish Church. It is the duty of the Deacon to help the Presbyter in divine worship, just as it was that of the Levite to help the Priest. And so with the consecration of the churches and the peculiar functions of ministers; they are all traceable to the fact that the construction of the early Church was left to Jews. Hence as the Jews used forms of prayer, so you find them used by the early Christians. Josephus, who was present at the siege of Jerusalem by Titus, declares, " that Christians in his time used prayers in their public worship, which they received from their forefathers." In the second century Justin Martyr says " We all rise and *in common* send up our prayers to God." Shortly after, Hippolytus, speaking of Antichrist says "when Antichrist shall come, Liturgies shall cease, singing of Psalms shall cease, and reading of Scriptures shall not be heard." I might weary you with similar quotations. There is no more doubt that the early Christian Church used forms of prayers, and forms exclusively in public worship, than there is that you are occupying those seats. The Bishop of each Church composed them for his diocese, so that although the same prayers were not used throughout the Church everywhere, yet every Church had its forms.

In conclusion, let us ask what can be said against this practice. Some call it *insincere*. " We never premeditate our speech," they say " when we are strongly affected. Prayer is the language of the heart, not of the head."—But what sort of a prayer, I would ask, would a man make, who did not use his brains ? Sincerity, it is very true, is the great requisite for prayer, but why should not a man be as sincere who uses a prayer that is written, as he who uses one that is not written! Prayer flows from a heart which the Spirit of God has made sensible of its needs, but will any one affirm that none are the subjects of divine grace who use forms? The heart right with God, whether it expresses its wants in the few and simple words of the Publican or in those of a Liturgy, is accepted of him. "God is a Spirit and they who worship Him" form or no form, " must worship Him in spirit and in truth." We do not contend that without the spirit of prayer there is any efficacy in a form.— We do not contend that the prayers of those who reject forms are not acceptable to God. We only maintain that forms of prayer are best adapted to public worship; and if we do not question the sincerity of those who differ from us, common charity requires that they should not question ours.

Again, some object to forms that *they confine prayer to what is written.* But to this I answer that, in the other way, prayer is confined to what is said. People cannot pray *together* unless they pray the same thing; and I can see no difference in point of liberty between joining in an extempore prayer and a precomposed one. You are tied down in both cases to what the speaker says, and I may well ask in the language of a Liturgical writer, "which would be the more preferable—that the prayer should be prepared for us by the well organized and systematic regulation of many wise and good men, with the Word of God before them for a guide, with the customs of antiquity for precedents, with due consideration, long discussion, every thought balanced, every word weighed ;—or that we should trust to the momentary effusions of an individual, who, however good, however able, however gifted he might be, could not at all times be said to be equal, and might from a thousand accidents fail either from bad memory, or from a want of readiness of expression, or inability at the very moment they might be wanted of seizing and applying in his requests of God, those topics which the sinfulness of man and the redemption of the world by the Son of God would claim at his hands."

Again, as to the objection *that we use a Prayer Book*, I would observe that most people, whether they use a Prayer Book or not in public worship, use Forms of Prayer. Do you suppose that the prayers offered in non-Episcopal churches are the offspring of the moment? Do you suppose that a Presbyterian Divine for instance, before going into his pulpit to conduct public worship, does not excogitate beforehand at least the nature and frequently the very words of his petitions? Do we not know that books have been written by those differing from us, to guide their ministers in this duty? Books wherein all the parts and order of a prayer, the Invocation, the Confession, the Praise, the Thanksgiving, the requests and the intercession, are laid down with elaborate care and method? And are not prayers thus systematized and premeditated as truly forms as if they were read out of a book? If not printed on paper, they are stamped on the mind, or memory. If they are not prepared for the occasion, still the matter of them is the result of study and reflection at some period of the speaker's life. They are to all intents and purposes forms, only they have not the advantage of being written forms. In our opinion the people cannot so well join in them, because ignorant of what the speaker is going to say. We think that accuracy and suitableness to the object is better secured by forms of prayer.

Finally, Brethren, let us adopt the language of the Apostle:— " I will pray with the spirit, and I will pray with the understanding also." You cannot otherwise adopt the petitions in the Prayer Book. To repeat its words is indeed formalism unless our hearts as well as our lips are engaged in the service. And doubtless there is the greatest danger of men committing the mockery of using our Prayer Book without meaning what they say. How solemn is the reflection that hundreds who would shrink from uttering such serious things as the Prayer Book contains, any where but in the Church, have no scruples about uttering them within its walls. Although they are living in sin and never pray at home, directly they enter the Church, they begin to say that they are "miserable sinners," and confess that they have erred and strayed like lost sheep. This is superstition or delusion, one of the two. Does a heartless prayer acquire an efficacy in the Church? Is it less sinful to say what you don't feel, inside than outside the Sanctuary? or is it not a greater insult to go into God's house, and do so?— May we all remember that formalism consists not in using our prayers, but in not being animated by the spirit of contrition, gratitude, faith, and love to Christ, which are their chief excellence and highest recommendation.

EXPOSITION

OF THE

MORNING SERVICE.

~~~~~~~~~~

" Let all things be done decently and in order."

I Cor. 14 : 40.

Having explained our reasons for using a form of prayer,* I shall in this, and the following lectures, go over all the parts of the morning service; for there are many things in it, which not only those who are strangers to our customs do not understand, but which many of our own people would be at a loss to account for. In public worship, we not only make known our requests to God, but we confess our sins to him, we praise him, and give him thanks; so that the transition from one of these acts, to another in our service, is the dividing point between them; and if we adopt for our lectures these natural divisions, the first will end with the Lord's prayer, where we pass from confession to praise; the second with the creed, where we change from praise to prayer, and the third will include the rest of the service.

By way of introduction I would observe that the intention of conducting the service decently and in order, is intimated by its very title, and that the first thing you meet with, is one of the directions interspersed through the prayer book to prevent disorder, and to guide both minister and people, in their respective parts.

---

* See Sermon 5.

They are called 'rubrics,' from a Latin word signifying *red*, because they were formerly printed in that colour. By attending to these rules, even a stranger on entering an Episcopal church, if he only knew where to find the Psalms, Collect, Litany, Communion, and Occasional Prayers, might join in our service as well as another. It is their not knowing where these may be found, that perplexes strangers. The minister passes suddenly from one part of the prayer book to another, and the uninitiated, at a loss to find the place, turn over the leaves with an embarrassed air, and perhaps secretly resolve to avoid placing themselves again in the like predicament.

The minister begins the Morning Prayer, by reading one or more *sentences of Scripture*. This is done to prepare the people for the solemn confession of their sins, to call their attention to the service, and to appeal to feelings such as they may be supposed to have brought with them into the house of God. There, men of all characters, and conditions congregate; the righteous, the ungodly, the penitent, the prodigal, the afflicted, the formalist, and the pharisee. You will find among these sentences something that applies to all of them. The righteous is taught to pray for a devotional frame of mind; the wicked are exhorted to turn from their wickedness; the penitent are consoled by the assurance that God will not despise a broken heart; the prodigal is warned to retrace his steps; the afflicted are enjoined to kiss the rod; the formalist is admonished to "rend his heart," and the pharisee not to rest in his fancied excellence. Now, is there not a manifest propriety in thus reminding all persons in what spirit, to be acceptable to God their prayers must be offered, in reminding them of the place in which they are, of the presence in which they stand, and of the object for which they are assembled? For the latter purpose, the first sentence is especially calculated. It always reminds me of the word 'Attention,' by which a regiment on the parade ground, is brought to order; "The Lord is in his holy temple; let all the earth keep silence before Him." This sentence was added by the American Church. It is not found in the English Liturgy, and it would be impossible to devise a finer opening than it is for public worship. It is not easy, even for serious men, busied all the week in secular affairs, to rid themselves when they enter a church of worldly thoughts. They will obtrude themselves even in the house of God. Alas! how many nominal Christians evince less reverence for the house of God than do Mahometans and Pagans for their mosques and temples. From the fact that idolaters, when converted to Christianity, conduct themselves so much better in a place of worship, than many who were born in a Christian land, there is cause to fear that the very commonness of the blessings and privileges of Christianity, to those who have never known any other religion, has the effect not as it ought, of making them respect the house of prayer, but of leading them on the contrary to look upon it very much as they look upon a court-house, town-hall, or any other public building. Speaking of the conduct of heathen converts in Ceylon, a missionary says, "that the women almost touched the ground with their heads as they knelt and engaged in prayer," and that "the men, kneeling upright, joined their hands, and closed their eyes with the simplicity of children." What a contrast, my friends, with the careless indifferent air, with which too many in this Christian country enter their pews! Well may we commence our service by reminding people that they are in the house of God, and should behave accordingly. "The Lord is in his holy temple; let all the earth keep silence before Him."

The last of these sentences leads directly to the *Exhortation*. It tells us that "if we confess our sins, God is faithful and just to forgive us our sins;" and then, that we may be induced to do this, the minister says that the confession of our sins to God, is not only often enjoined in Scripture, but that their concealment, or extenuation, is expressly forbidden. He adds however, that it must not be the confession of the lips only, but of "an humble, lowly, penitent, and obedient heart." These are the signs of a true repentance; shame, humiliation, sorrow on account of sin, and above all, reform. Such confession, proper at all times, the minister tells the people, is especially so in view of the acts of worship for which they are assembled, and having thus prepared the way for it, he invites them to accompany him in "the general confession." But before proceeding with this, I am reminded both by his asking them to do so audibly, and by its being required in the rubric to be said "kneeling," that this is the proper place to make a few remarks on the responses, and upon the posture which we adopt in prayer.

The Responses. These are those parts of the service which the people are required to say aloud. The tongue can never be so well employed as in worshipping God. It is called "man's glory" in the Scriptures, because it puts it in his power to glorify God in a way peculiar to himself, in a way of which no other creature is capable. The stars glorify him by the silent grandeur with which they obey his laws, and by displaying his attributes, all his works praise him. But the power of speech, enables man to glorify God by expressing the emotions which the view of his works awaken in the mind of a rational being; it is therefore of essential use in rendering him a reasonable worship. Moreover, the attention of the people is kept alive, by having a share in the service. "I prefer the prayer book," said a sailor, "because the minister does not reserve all the speaking to himself." There is much philosophy in keeping the congregation actively employed, and when they join in the service with one accord, they realize the idea of public worship. Go into a church where the people really unite in praise, and prayer; and then enter another, where these duties are performed

by a few scattered, languid voices, and how much more animating
is the effect in the one, than in the other! In the first, you feel
that the people actuated by the same spirit, are praying to God like
one man, while in the last, with the exception of two or three, they
appear not to be praying at all. I would observe also that the meaning of our service is obscure without the responses. Gaps occur
in the sense of it, when the part assigned to the people is dropped,
or slurred over. In the psalter, for instance, each verse does not
always include a period, so that unless the people continue the sentence which the minister begins, he has to commence another, while
the foregoing one is incomplete. To bring out the meaning, and
beauty of the service, there must be wherever it is required, an
audible, reverent and fervent response. The charge of formality,
and lifelessness made against us, is greatly owing to the apparent
want of spirituality arising from neglect in these particulars, and
really it is a great injustice to our church, to give any such reason
of censure to her enemies. I have known persons blamed by those
in the next pew, for responding audibly, but the fact is that they
ought to have responded audibly themselves. It certainly is a dis-
turbance to persons engaged in *silent* prayer, for people to speak
aloud by the side of them, but what right have we to complain of
that in an Episcopal Church, where no one is expected to hold his
tongue? Ours is a united worship, and you might as well find fault
with the choir for singing so as to be heard, as with the worshipper
for speaking audibly, since the responsive character of the service
would be lost otherwise. Some object to the confused effect of a
number of voices, and no doubt if it were not supposed that all are
provided with prayer books, and join in the service, it might be
difficult to understand what is said, but the use of the Liturgy ob-
viates this objection; and as to the rest, the effect is sublime.—
It is " like the voice of many waters," the very sound to which St.

John compares the worship of heaven. The roar of the cataract, the raging of the sea, and the rushing of the wind are confused sounds, but how grand they are; so is the sound of many voices, ascending to heaven in praise and prayer.

The Confession is to be said *kneeling*, as the most becoming outward sign of reverence and humiliation. I do not say that such feelings may not exist where no such homage is rendered. Nor do I say that prayer is not effectual unless offered in a kneeling posture; but I ask whether a man who addresses the great God of heaven and earth upon his knees, does not give a better outward evidence than he could otherwise, of his deep sense of God's majesty, and of his own unworthiness? We think that he does, and we refer you in proof of it, both to the sanction which the opinion derives from the general sentiment of mankind, and from the testimony of the word of God. The way in which men have expressed their opinion on this subject, is by adopting the custom either of kneeling or prostrating themselves wherever great reverence is intended. We all know to what a humiliating degree this homage is rendered in eastern countries, but it is the usage of the most civilized courts in Europe, to this day, to bow the knee to the Sovereign. Indeed this is the way in which men are apt to express their admiration of power, or their submission to authority, or their deference to rank, or their earnestness in petition everywhere; and therefore it is perhaps, that where in Scripture the universal dominion of Christ is spoken of, it is said "every knee shall bow to him." It was no doubt in accordance with the dictates of nature, that so many people while supplicating Christ whilst he was on earth, assumed this posture. "There came a leper to him beseeching him, and kneeling down to him, and saying unto him, if thou wilt thou canst make me clean." Again, "there came one running, and kneeled to him, and asked him, "Good master, what shall I do that I may inherit eternal life?" So it was with the father of the lunatic St. Matthew speaks of. He came to Jesus "kneeling down to him, and saying, Lord have mercy on my son." And so it was even with St. Peter himself, after he had witnessed one of Christ's most stupendous miracles. He "fell down at Jesus' knees, saying depart from me for I am a sinful man, O Lord." I think you will admit from these instances, that the sentiment of mankind is decidedly in favour of kneeling, as "that posture of humility, in which the body most naturally expresses the supplication of the mind." Even the Mahometan, on hearing the call to prayer, instinctively casts himself on his knees, and begins his devotions. But kneeling has been consecrated by some of the highest authorities in the Bible, as the attitude of prayer. Solomon "kneeled down upon his knees" at the consecration of the temple. Daniel prayed three times a day in this posture, and David says "Let us kneel before the Lord our Maker." Nor can it be objected that this was done only under the old dispensation, for in the New Testament, we find that St. Peter and St. Paul, and even our Lord himself, who is our example wherever we can copy him, kneeled when they prayed to God.— Even if man were innocent, since the holy angels fall down before God, it would not become one inferior to the angels to do less; but that a fallen being should retain in addressing the Almighty an erect posture, as if he were spiritually upright, and sinless, is highly improper. He ought to kneel, if it were but to show his shameful consciousness of having fallen from his high estate. It was an observation of Frederic the Third, that "the forms used by Protestants in divine service, made them appear to worship one not superior to themselves;" but it seems to us, that to stand or sit in prayer, wears the look of worshipping one inferior to ourselves. How would you construe it if a man on your calling upon him,

B

were not to rise when you entered his apartment? Would you not conclude that he held you in light esteem? Is it possible then to regard it otherwise than a cool, disrespectful indifference, such as men are apt to exhibit to those beneath them, when on coming into God's presence, instead of falling on their knees, they assume the easiest and most familiar posture? In making these remarks, we intend only to justify our own practice, although in doing so we seem to condemn others. Episcopalians themselves, are often neglectful about kneeling in prayer. Some simply incline the head on the back of the pew opposite to them, and even so much reverence as this is withheld by others. From this neglect, to a looker-on the appearance of a congregation must be strange indeed. He sees some asleep, with their faces half covered by their hands, and others surveying those in their vicinity. Nothing shews more the propriety of kneeling in prayer, than the indecorum, and levity, and incongruousness, which arise from not doing so. Even the Presbyterians are attending to this subject, for I saw it stated in a recent number of the Episcopal Recorder, that the Rev. Mr. Caird, of the Scotch Church, has recently urged it earnestly on his people "to kneel during prayer, and to stand during singing." If this be the case it is high time for Churchmen to reform their neglect in these particulars.

Now we come to *the Confession* itself. It is the language of one profoundly sensible of his guilt and weakness, truly desirous of pardon, and fully resolved by God's grace to forsake sin. In short it is the language of evangelical repentance, and affords a good instance of the care with which doctrinal error is guarded against in the prayer book. It holds out no hope to a man of recovering himself " by his own natural strength" from sin and misery, nor does it ask either for pardon or for grace to help us to do better, except through the promises of God, and the merits of Christ.—

And you will observe that it is not a confession to the Priest. The rubric says that the priest must kneel down and confess his sins, as well as the people, although to prevent confusion they are to follow him in doing so. They are not to whisper their confession in the ear of a priest, but they are to say it audibly in the church, for it is to God only, as the offended party, that confession is due. This, you will readily imagine, was never derived from the Church of Rome. The Introductory sentence, Exhortation, Confession, and Absolution were all added by the Reformers, when the Liturgy was revised and republished in 1552, and that revision was chiefly owing to the complaint of Calvin, Bucer, and others, that the prayer book as it was at first in Edward the Sixth's reign, was still too superstitious. The fact is that the Liturgy of the Church of England put on her Protestant attire gradually. To drop her Romish garb all at once, was impossible; and it is curious to observe how for sixteen years, it passed through divers refining processes, and came out more Protestant than it was before, from each of them. Were the first book of Edward the Sixth now in use, we should call the Communion the Mass, Mary Magdalen a Saint, we should have prayers for the dead; the "Lord's table" would be "the altar." We should anoint the confirmed, make the sign of the cross in matrimony, and attire our Bishops and Presbyters in other vestments. Never countenance those who would bring our Church nearer to what she was when in communion with the Church of Rome. The safest charioteer, Bishop Chase used to say, is he who drives as far as possible from the edge of a precipice, not he who tries how near he can approach it without upsetting.

But what is this, you will say "The declaration of *Absolution* or Remission of Sins to be made by the Priest alone ?" Do Episcopalians believe that Ministers can forgive sins? They believe that ministers are empowered to declare that sins may be forgiven, and that where there are true repentance and faith, they are forgiven. This is the Gospel, because upon these conditions only, can the benefits of Christ's death be had; and if ministers are not authorized to declare this, how are they to fulfil the command to "preach the Gospel to every creature"? It is indispensable to the discharge of their commission, that they should be competent to declare on what terms God will pardon a sinner. They could neither point out the way of salvation otherwise, nor console those who are converted to God. It is plain from the rubric, that nothing more than this is intended; plainer in our rubric, than in that of the Church of England, for what is called only a "declaration" in ours, in the other is styled "the absolution or remission of sins." It was, however, for the express purpose of showing that the word "absolution" is not used in the Romish sense, that the words "remission of sins," were added. It was done at the instance of the Puritans. The whole spirit of our Liturgy contradicts the idea that a priest can forgive sins; and in fact in "the absolution" itself, the priest disclaims any such power, for after telling the people that he is authorized to assure the penitent of forgiveness, how does he assure them of it? By telling them that not "he," the priest, but God "pardoneth and absolveth all those who truly repent, and unfeignedly believe his holy Gospel." It would be strange indeed, if after claiming authority to tell the people that God absolved the penitent from their sins, he were to pretend to forgive them himself. Besides, this form of absolution came from a source which will not be suspected of favouring Popery. "The Liturgy used by one of the reformers in Germany is in almost the same words," and I have read that the idea of putting the "absolution" here at all was suggested to the Church of England by Calvin saying in one of his works, "There is not one of us who does not acknowledge it to be most useful, that with public confession should be joined some striking promise, which may excite sinners to the hope of pardon and reconciliation." I observe too that "Archbishop Lawrence in his Bampton Lectures says, that the sentences, Exhortation, Confession, and Absolution were in some degree taken from Calvin's Liturgy." These considerations are quite enough to acquit us of believing in priestly absolution.

Whilst the Minister is delivering the message he has received from God, the people are told to continue kneeling. Does it not strike you as proper that they should receive such a message on their knees? Is it not in accordance with a sense of unworthiness and gratitude, which such a mark of God's condescension and goodness should occasion? If a pardoned criminal throws himself at the feet of the Executive, to express his overwhelming obligations for his clemency, ought not a sinner saved from hell, to receive the tidings of his deliverance in the humblest posture? The Minister it is true, stands, while the people kneel in this part of the service, but it is because he is speaking with authority as God's ambassador. If not officiating, he would kneel likewise, and in the Confession, you will remember, that as their fellow sinner, he takes the same posture with themselves; but when in his character as God's messenger, he makes this declaration, he very properly stands up out of regard to the relative position of the people and himself. An ambassador must be careful not to compromise the dignity of his sovereign. He must, as his representative, act as the sovereign would do himself, and therefore the minister, when he declares God's forgiveness of the penitent, assumes the attitude most significant of the authority, power, and majesty of his master. The people, in this part of the service are silent. It is to be said "by the Priest alone," although I have known persons to join in it, for want of comprehending the principles upon which the rubric directs

the contrary. It is the Minister who is here speaking to the people,
and nothing but ignorance can induce them to take part in what is
addressed to themselves. There are prayers indeed wherein no
voice is to be audible but the Minister's; still even in them the
people are to unite mentally. Protestants believe in no mediator but
Christ, between God and man, and therefore, although the Minister
conducts their devotions, he does not pray in the stead of the people.
The only Priest who offers our prayers to God, and who by his office
gives them efficacy, is He "who is set on the right hand of the throne
in the Majesty in the heavens." As the priest therefore only leads their
devotions, the people are to follow him in their minds, even in those
prayers where the Church thinks it most conducive to order that
they should be silent. But "the Absolution" is not a prayer, and
all they have to do is to listen while it is being pronounced, and to
say "*amen*" at its conclusion. They are to say Amen not only
there, but "at the end of every prayer," because it signifies their
acquiescence in what the Minister says, and that they heartily
concur in the petitions. Some pronounce the *a* in this word like
that in *far*, and no doubt in the Greek it has that sound, but all
words naturalized from a foreign tongue into ours, do not on that
account retain the sound which they had where they came from.
Walker, who says that "Custom is the sovereign arbiter of languages," and Worcester, with many other authorities, assign to the
first letter of the word 'amen' the sound which it bears in the
English alphabet. Which of these two is most in accordance with
general usage, you can judge for yourselves. For my own part, I
look upon it as a piece of affectation, to call a word one way in
the Church, and another out of it. In the ears of a man of sense,
words acquire no weight from their sound apart from their suitableness, and since they are better understood when they are pronounced the common way, that seems to be the preferable one.—

" Amen" usually signifies in the Prayer Book " so be it." It comes from the Hebrew, and is used assentingly in the twenty-seventh chapter of Deuteronomy; but at the end of the Creed it is rather an assertion than a mere assent. When we say amen to the articles of our belief, we strongly affirm our faith in them.

But to return; now suppose a man sincerely penitent for his sins appropriates the Declaration we have been speaking of, what in your opinion would his feelings lead him to do? We know that " out of the abundance of the heart the mouth speaketh," how then do you suppose that a man lately burdened with fears, and accusations, but now filled with peace and joy in believing, would express himself? Would he not be prompted at once to draw nigh to God as a reconciled father in Christ Jesus? Would it not be in accordance with his character as a child of God, as no longer an alien, but a member by adoption and grace of his family, to make known to God his requests, and ask Him to shield him from danger, to deliver him from evil, and to provide for his support? On this ground it is that *Prayer* follows the Absolution. The devotional part of the service indeed is in another place, but as the first words which a pardoned sinner utters should be those of prayer, it is so ordered. And *The Lord's Prayer*, because the fact that Christ was its author, entitles it to be the first prayer in the service. It would not be respectful to put any other prayer before that of Christ. This feeling was so strong formerly, that most of the old Liturgies begin with the Lord's prayer, and indeed that was the case at first with the Prayer Book of the Church of England. Even an American clergyman may use the Lord's prayer three times in the morning service if he pleases. This is actually done in the Church of England, but considering that its repetition is owing to to the union of three distinct services, the Morning Prayer, Litany, and Communion Service, our reviewers have made its use more than once optional with the Minister. The propriety of using it after the Absolution, is apparent from the fact that the Lord's prayer is the prayer of God's family on earth, and so more proper than any other for one just admitted or restored to its privileges. If we were not in these Lectures explaining rather the order of our service than its theology, we might show that this prayer is unsuited to an unconverted man, because he is an utter stranger to its spirit. He lacks the filial feeling, the love of holiness, the anxiety for Christ's second coming, the spirit of obedience, and submission, and dependence, the dread of temptation and zeal for God's glory, which are breathed in it. O may we have the feelings that corresponds with its requests, the spirit that can say Amen to its petitions. It is one thing to say a thousand 'pater nosters' with the lips, and quite another with the heart of a child of God, a new creature in Christ Jesus to cry "Abba" Father.

EXPOSITION

OF THE

MORNING SERVICE.

~~~~~~~~~~

" Let all things be done decently and in order."

I Cor. 14: 40.

The people have now confessed their sins, and have been assured
that if penitent they are forgiven; but it does not follow that they
can appropriate the comfort of that assurance, and exchange at
once their sighs of contrition for songs of praise. Many persons
are so much affected by a sense of their sins that they persist in
spite of all assurance to the contrary in saying that they have sinned
beyond forgiveness. They need to be enabled to lay hold by faith
of the great truth that "the blood of Christ cleanseth from all sin."
It is not the mere assurance that God will forgive the penitent
that can console and fill their hearts with joy, but the faith whereby a comfortable hope is drawn from that assurance, that they are
forgiven. In the absence of this they must continue kneeling at
the throne of grace, without the power of uttering aught but the
publican's prayer, "God have mercy on me a sinner," or that of
the disciples, "Lord save us, or we perish." How can they sing
praises to God, until relieved by a sense of his favour from the burden of their guilt and misery? Therefore, the minister goes on to
say, *" O Lord open thou our lips."* Give the heavy laden sinners

before Thee such a sense of thy pardon that unable to contain themselves they may break forth into singing to express their joy. So the words may be paraphrased, and so the people seem to under-stand them, for they complete the sentence "and our mouth will show forth thy praise." They are the words of David, when for his sins God had hidden his face from him; and although his offences were very aggravated, there are none of us who when we remember our sins, should not have our lips sealed by shame until God open them by forgiveness.

And now, the Service proceeds upon the supposition that this prayer is answered, that God has given to the people "the oil of joy, for mourning, and the garment of praise for the spirit of heaviness;" and so they are directed to rise from their knees, and stand up, for although until pardoned, they were like the publican, and could not so much as look up to heaven, yet now being reconciled and about to engage in praising God, a standing posture is as proper for them as a kneeling one was before. If the one implies lowliness of heart, so does the other exaltation of soul. If the one is significant of humility, so is the other of joy. The first expression of this which they utter on rising from their knees is *The Doxology*. The minister exclaims "Glory be to the Father and to the Son and to the Holy Ghost." I look upon the Doxology here as equivalent to saying "Thank God!" words in which the heart spontaneously expresses its feelings on escaping danger.— See how naturally the sailor exclaims "thank God!" when he is rescued from a watery grave. What else would the manslayer say as he gained the shelter of the city of refuge? and what else should the people say, who are now supposed through repentance and faith to have received pardon, and to have escaped the condem-nation of those who are out of Christ? But why, you may ask, is there so much prolixity about this ascription? Would it not suffice to say "Glory be to the Father and to the Son and to the Holy Ghost, now and ever, world without end?" Why should we add "as it was in the beginning!" These words were added to assert our belief that the Son is co-eternal with the Father. Our doxology at first was little more than "Glory be to the Father and to the Son and to the Holy Ghost," but when it was said by heretics that Christ was created by the Father, that he was no more than the first of created beings, and that there was a time when he had no exist-ence, the doxology was made to confront these falsehoods; to express not only the present and future, but the previous existence of Christ, that he was in the beginning "with God, and therefore that he is himself God." Thus Brethren, our prayers are chronicles of the conflicts which the Church has fought on its march onward.

And now the Doxology concluded, what shall follow? Shall not the people unite in praising God? It is written, "Whoso offereth praise glorifieth me," and after professing so much zeal for God's glory, the following anthem is the natural expression of the feelings by which the people are now supposed to be actuated. They are supposed to have repented, to have believed and to be forgiven, and were they to hold their peace "the stones would cry out." No sooner therefore, does the minister invite them, saying "Praise ye the Lord," than they answer "The Lord's name be praised," and unite at once in the Anthem "O come, Let us sing unto the Lord, let us heartily rejoice in the strength of our salvation." You may say perhaps, that 'were they all believers this would be very beau-tiful.' There are unbelievers, no doubt, in all congregations. To the all-seeing eye of God "not every one who saith unto Him, 'Lord, Lord," belongs to His kingdom. But the Church is neither able nor authorized to discern between the wheat and the tares.—

To be consistent with herself she must make her services coincide with her character as a "congregation of faithful men." She puts such language into the lips of those who worship in her sanctuaries therefore, as corresponds with what they ought to be. Her prayers would be strangely miscalled Church prayers otherwise.

Before the Anthem there is a rubric, which allows the 'Venite' either to be said or sung, but in certain cases prohibits its use. These are first "when other anthems are appointed," as on Easter day for instance. Again on Christmas day, Ash Wednesday, Good Friday, Ascension day and Whitsunday, if instead of using the proper psalms for those days, the minister chooses to adopt one of the Selections, he is obliged to substitute certain psalms which are at the end of the selections in place of the 'Venite.' It is also dispensed with in the "Form of prayer for the visitation of Prisoners," and in that of "Thanksgiving to Almighty God for the Fruits of the Earth." In these instances other psalms being appointed, the 'Venite' is to be omitted.

The rubric also directs its omission when the Anthem occurs in the Psalter; for being mostly taken from the 95th Psalm, there would be a needless repetition of it on the nineteenth day of the month otherwise. Many ministers, however, since the least deviation from the ordinary routine of the Service is embarrassing, avoid the omission of the 'Venite' on that day, by availing themselves of the right to substitute for the psalms in regular course, one of the Selections.

The Venite is called "the Invitatory Psalm" because the people are invited in it to join in the praises and prayers, which are now about to be offered to the Almighty. And here I am reminded that strangers imagine our Service to be a kind of medley, a collection of remnants tacked together without any natural connection. In the place assigned to our hymns, prayers, psalms and lessons, they see no design to make of them one harmonious whole. But it is a great beauty of our Service, that there is a dependence among all its parts. The 'Venite' is an introduction to all the subsequent acts of worship; to the psalms, the lessons, the prayers, the confessions of faith. What idea does it embody? That those whose sins God has forgiven will not only celebrate his praise themselves, but call upon their fellow men to join with them, "O come, let us sing unto the Lord." To this invitation the Psalms are responsive.

But we must speak of *The Psalms* in connection with the rubric that relates to them. "Then shall follow a portion of the Psalms as they are appointed." This refers to the Psalter. You will find directions for its use at the beginning of the Prayer Book. There are psalms appointed for thirty days in a month, morning and evening. If it happen to be the thirty-first day of any month, the psalms for the thirtieth day are to be repeated. But before the Psalter there are selections of Psalms which may be "used instead of those for the day, at the discretion of the minister." These selections are not found in the Liturgy of the Church of England. They were designed to avoid the necessity of reading what are called the "imprecatory psalms," as well as those which because not adapted "to the general circumstances and state of mind of a mixed congregation" are less suited than others for public worship. Passages of the psalms from which these Selections are taken are omitted, and they were objected to on this and on other grounds by Bishop White at the time of their adoption. He favoured the plan of permitting the minister to select such psalms from the whole Psalter as he might see fit, because he thought that some would consider the rejec-

tion of a portion of holy writ "on a supposed unfitness for any act
of Christian devotion" as taking an unwarranted liberty with the
Word of God. You may have observed, that the sixth, and the
third Selections, are more used than the others which are very
lengthy, but if they were all brief, or if the discretion recommended
by Bishop White were accorded to ministers, it is very doubtful
whether the daily arrangement, after all, would not be preferred by
the Church at large.

The Prayer Book version of the Psalms is different from that in
our present translation of the Bible. Its language is more diffuse
but more musical. Which sounds the sweetest—to say "Which
turned the rock into a standing water, the flint into a fountain of
waters," or to say "who turned the hard rock into a standing water
and the flint stone into a springing well"?—Or take that description
of a good man in the first psalm, and which has most harmony in
it—"He shall be like a tree planted by the rivers of water," or
"He shall be like a tree planted by the water side"? or in the
third verse,—"The ungodly are not so," the Bible has it, "but
are like the chaff which the wind driveth away." How much more
sweetly it is said in the Prayer Book, "As for the ungodly, it is
not so with them; but they are like the chaff which the wind scattereth away from the face of the earth." The word "scattereth"
expresses the effect of the wind upon chaff much better than "driveth." The Prayer Book version of the Psalms is derived from the
Bible printed in England in 1539, and for its sweetness of translation was retained in the Liturgy, although the Epistles and Gospels
and afterwards the Lessons were on its revision taken from the
Bible of James the First.

St. Paul speaks of the use of "psalms, hymns, and spiritual
songs" in public worship, and these Psalms of David have been so

used from age to age, both by Jews and Christians. Pliny, a heathen writer, speaks of the practice as that of the Christians of his
day, and wherever the apostolic model of a church is found, it
prevails still. What a tribute to the excellence of the Psalms of
David! They furnish the Christian in prosperity and in tribulation,
in joy and in sorrow, in sickness and in health, in time of temptation and in the hour of death with words adapted both to his condition and feelings. How many broken and contrite hearts in the
house of God have been consoled by them!

Neither in our Rubric nor in that of the Church of England is
any thing said of the manner of performing this part of the Service.
In England the custom is to sing the Psalms in Cathedrals, and
to say them in parish churches; but as the first method confines
this important part to the choir, it is less adapted than the other to
public worship. It may be consistent with the "ancient practice of
the Greek and Latin Church," but it is not edifying, and to many
persons it is positively injurious to have only to listen while "one
side of the choir sing one verse and the other side another" of the
Psalms. By joining in them they are much more likely to understand, to feel, to appropriate, and to make David's language their
own. As for the plea that the angels sing in this way in heaven, it
may be admitted when the Church on earth, like that in heaven,
forms one choir, and when its members, like the angels, are under
no temptation to think more of how they sing than of what is sung.

The Rubric goes on to say, that "at the end of every Psalm,"
and after certain Anthems in the Morning and Evening Service, the
Doxology may be sung. In the Church of England, to use the
Doxology after every Psalm, is imperative; but here it is only obli-
gatory to use it after "the whole portion or selection of Psalms for

B

the day." In very few of our parishes comparatively is it used after each separate psalm, although to this we have no objection, except that were the one or the other practice general, there would be more uniformity in our churches. I wish that every thing as to the mode of performing divine service were prescribed, ordered, and made imperative, so that Episcopalians might find themselves as much at home in one of our sanctuaries as in another, might find in any one of them throughout the country precisely the same customs as in his parish church. Even the clergy, by the difference of usage, are often unable from conscientious scruples to adopt each others' fashions, while should they exchange, they feel a delicacy as to retaining their own. It is not calculated to allay the acrimony of party spirit to adopt peculiarities in the mode of worship as outward badges of opinion. On the contrary, it is calculated to exacerbate its rancour and to widen the breach which yawns already like a great gulf between churchmen of opposite views. Besides, if we were obliged to use *no other ceremonies* but what the Church prescribes would it not hinder the growth among us of such as were discarded by the Church of England, and of which she says that "because they were winked at in the beginning they grew daily to more and more abuses." If things go on as they do at present, we shall have as many ways of performing the Church Service as there are dioceses, nay as many as there are diversities of sentiment.

The reason commonly assigned for using the Doxology after the Psalms, is that it proclaims the God therein spoken of, to be the same triune God whom Christians worship, and so explains the use in our churches, of what under the old dispensation, was part of the temple service. But there is another reason. It ascribes glory by name to each person in the Trinity and thus supplies what the Christian feels the want of in the Psalms of David; for neither in

them nor in the anthems is there any mention of the persons in the
Godhead, so that the Doxology in those praises to which it is sub-
joined is designed to supply an omission. This is plain from its
not being used after the 'Te Deum' because in that there is no such
omission.—The 'Gloria in Excelsis' may be used in place of the
'Gloria Patri' after the Psalms, although in the English Prayer
Book, this grand ascription of praise, which is 1700 years old, is
reserved to the close of the Communion Service. Certainly no language could better speak the emotions of a grateful heart. See
how the Church labours in it to express her sense of obligation to
God. It seems as if she would employ all the riches of language and
yet finds them all inadequate. "We praise thee, we bless thee, we
worship thee, we glorify thee, we give thanks to thee." It reminds
us of the ascription of angels in heaven, "Blessing, and glory, and
wisdom, and thanksgiving, and honour, and power and might be
unto our God for ever and ever, amen." Indeed, much of the
'Gloria in Excelsis' is taken from the hymnal of angels, for it
begins with the song which they sung on Christ's birth-day, and the
lips of the man who wrote it must have been touched with a coal
from the angels' altar. It flames with love. There can be no doxology without love.

> " Without it, vile are myrrh and gold,
> And vain the swell of soaring word,
> For He who can our thought behold
> A loveless prayer has never heard."

We are now to speak of *the Lessons*, because at this point of the
Service the Word of God is read to the people. Now they assume
the attitude of disciples or learners, who always sat at their Instruc-
tor's feet. There is no order for it in the rubric, but it is sufficiently indicated to the people by the fact that they have nothing

to do but listen; besides which, as up to this point in the Service they have been in a standing or kneeling posture, they require rest. The reading of the Holy Scriptures, even were it only out of respect to their divine Author, should have a prominent place in public worship. But it tends to cherish a reverence for the sacred volume; it gives to the ignorant some knowledge of its contents; it makes even those who search the Scriptures more familiar with them, and it helps hearers to understand sermons, and to detect false doctrine. Above all, it is a means of grace which God has attended with his richest blessing. How many instances might be mentioned of lasting religious impressions being received through hearing the Scripture read in Church. That our Liturgy is so thoroughly imbued with Scripture, that so much of it is read in the Psalms, Epistles, Gospels and Lessons is one of its capital excellencies. This practice has obtained in the Church of God, under both dispensations, but at the time of the Reformation the lessons were so mingled with passages from human writings, anecdotes of saints, &c., that even if they had not been in a foreign tongue the people could not have been much the better for them. In allusion to this it is said in the preface to the English prayer book, that "nothing is ordained to be read but the very pure word of God, the Holy Scriptures." Great was the joy of the people of England when they heard the Bible read in the churches in their native tongue. How it must have opened their eyes to the corruptions of the Church of Rome! One reason, perhaps, why a daily service was appointed, was to give the people who had been debarred from it an opportunity of becoming familiar with the Bible. And not only the people but the clergy likewise, for they were ordered to read the morning and evening service every day on purpose, the preface says, that they might be better acquainted with the word of

God. Now it is true, that both by their education and the general circulation of the Scriptures there is not the same reason for it, but the public reading of the Bible in churches will always be a safeguard from error, and a source of instruction and a means of grace.

It may be thought, perhaps, because there are lessons appointed for every day in the year, and a morning and evening service in the American Prayer Book, that it was intended to have daily worship in our churches, but there is no legislation to sustain that inference, and perhaps for the very good reason that all legislation in England on the subject has proved nugatory. So few attended daily service in England, that Wheatly says the Priest had often to say prayers by himself, and on that account it was ordered that if he could not get a congregation he must say them in his own family. So ended the attempt in England to impose daily service on the people, and profiting by this experience, our Church leaves her ministers to act in this matter according to circumstances. They who dispense with a daily service in the exercise of the liberty thus accorded to them, have as much law on their side as those who do otherwise, although the latter unhappily are apt to plume themselves upon having daily prayers, as more righteous and as better churchmen than their neighbours, whom they affect either to pity for their ignorance, or to despise for their laxity.

The Hymns which succeed the Lessons denote that the people receive the Scriptures with joy and gratitude. This feeling is manifested in the 'Te Deum,' by praising God for the truths revealed in them, such as the Trinity, the Incarnation, the Atonement; but at the same time this noble hymn, in which all created intelligences seem with one voice to praise God, is suited as an expression of gratitude to all occasions.

The 'Te Deum,' was written, it is said, as far back at least as the fourth century, and nothing equal to it has been composed since. It is, perhaps, the most magnificent tribute of the kind which, without the inspiration of the Holy Ghost, was ever written. And with what interesting associations is it connected! Many a victory by land and sea; many a deliverance from foe and famine, plague and pestilence, has been celebrated in cathedrals and in camps, in parish churches, and in navies by this sublime ascription of glory to God. Of course the doxology is never used after it. It would be superfluous.— There is another 'Canticle' which may be substituted for the 'Te Deum' after the first lesson, 'The Benedicite.' On Thanksgiving occasions it is particularly appropriate. The hymn after the second lesson, the hundredth Psalm, and the song of Simeon, require no comment, and therefore I shall close my remarks for the present, reserving the consideration of the Apostles' Creed until the next occasion.

EXPOSITION

OF THE

MORNING SERVICE.

~~~~~~~~~~~

" Let all things be done decently and in order."

I Cor. 14 : 40.

THE APOSTLES' CREED.

In resuming our remarks on the Morning Service, we commence with the rubric prefixed to the Apostles' Creed. It directs the use of it *in this place ;* that is, after the hymn which follows the second lesson. But why there particularly? Has the Church any special reason for assigning the Creed to this, rather than to any other part of the Service? I would remind you in reply of what we have been engaged in. We have been reading the Scriptures, and praising God for giving them to us; this is the place, therefore, for professing our belief in their contents. The subject matter of the Bible, from Genesis to Revelation, is God, as Creator, Redeemer, Sanctifier, and man as a sinner. Now, in the Creed the doctrines of the Bible on these points are condensed. Its repetition, therefore, here, is as much as to say, ' I believe all that the book which has just been read, contains.' Besides, as the prayers follow the Creed, its repetition here is proper as a profession of faith in the God we pray to, in the Saviour through whose merits our prayers are offered, and in the Holy Ghost, who teaches us how to pray. It is a proper introduction, therefore, not only to the prayers before the Litany, which are all offered in the name of Jesus, but to the Litany itself, in which the persons of the Trinity are severally invoked in the most solemn manner. It also reminds the congregation, of facts well calculated to lead them to join heartily in the ensuing prayers, such as a future state, the resurrection from the dead, a judgment to come, and forgiveness of sins. If any considerations can prepare them to engage in this solemn duty, these are the most serious and soul-stirring ones that the mind can dwell upon.

The rubric tells us next, that in saying the Creed, the whole Church, minister and people, should unite their voices. Just as they do in the General Confession, and for the same reason. There is nothing in the Creed peculiar to my faith or yours particularly. It is our common faith. As we confess our sins together, because we are all sinners, so we say the Creed together, because it contains nothing but what we all believe. And then the *attitude* is mentioned. It is to be said standing. Why?—Because that posture accords best with the nature of the act. This may be illustrated by an English phrase of great significance, "To stand to a thing" is to adhere to it, to persist in its assertion. "To stand by a man" is to be his friend and maintain his cause. Such expressions show that men agree in thinking a standing posture to denote firmness, resolve, determination, and hence to imply our attachment to the articles of our faith, and our resolve to contend for them, we rehearse them standing. The custom came down to us from men who lived when had they been detected in saying the Creed, they would have lost their life. If we are not called as they often were, to prove the stedfastness of our faith, by holding fast to it in the flames, still the same mind should be in us which was in them, and in that case, standing up when we say the Creed has lost none of its significance by the lapse of time.

II.—As to what is said in the rubric of Christ's descent into hell, I will speak of that presently. Let us now attend to our *reason for using the Apostles' Creed in public worship*.

It is an *old custom*, that is one reason. On my admiring a hymn the other day at a friend's house, he told me that it was an old family hymn—that for generations back it had been the family favourite. Who will say that the value which the hymn derived to him from that circumstance was unmerited? If we attach a value to any article because it was used by our forefathers, why should we not for the same reason venerate their hymns and their confessions of faith? We should think it very unfeeling for a man to discard the old arm chair which his mother occupied, to make room for furniture of a later fashion; and would it not be equally so for Churchmen to reject as antiquated the forms which their ancestors used in public worship. Could you substitute better ones it would make a difference; but ancient as they are, nothing so beautiful or so well adapted to their purpose has appeared since.— Where will you find, within so small a compass, so full and comprehensive an epitome of Christian doctrine as is contained in the Apostles' Creed? We may freely indulge our feelings therefore, in regard to it, as the Creed of our ancestors. Without asserting, as some do, that the Apostles wrote it, still, as a summary of their doctrines it deserves its name. Parts of it are quoted by men who lived not long after the Apostles, and it is so old that, if not theirs, we are at a loss to know whence it came. As you can tell by its rude material and workmanship that the arrow head of flintstone belonged to a primitive people; so the simplicity of the Apostles' Creed denotes its age. It is said to have been the watchword of the primitive Christians—the countersign by which they distinguished friend from foe. It was "the sign or mark" by which they knew believers from infidels. It was their test of orthodoxy, their

rule of faith. Is it any wonder that we should adhere to a form
which has been thus consecrated? If you love the old family hymn
which tradition tells you your ancestors for generations past appre-
ciated, should we not love the old Creed which our Church ancestors
have so highly prized in past ages? Birds of a feather might as
soon cease to sing the same song, as Churchmen of the 19th century
cease to use the same Creed as those of the first.

2.) Again, *it helps to maintain sound doctrine*. It has always
been put by the Church to this use. From age to age, as heresies
sprung up, articles were added to the Creed in testimony against
them. The article of Christ's descent into hell, in the Apostles'
Creed was put there on that account. Heretics denied that Christ
had a human soul. They said that his divine nature united to his
body was in place of a soul. Then the Church inserted this in the
Creed that he descended into hell, for that proved him to have a
human soul, since his body was in the grave, and his divine nature
every where, so that unless he had a human soul he could not have
descended into hell at all. Bishop White says that in the Revolution
when from various causes the Episcopal Church was on the decline,
and when most of its sanctuaries were closed, devotion was kept
alive in domestic circles by the use of the Liturgy. In the same
way may it be said that the knowledge of the true faith has been
preserved by the use of the Creed in churches. Can you doubt
that its use in our own Church has contributed to that end? Parents
are charged to teach it to their children. Sponsors are obliged to
confess their faith in it. Without knowing it no adult can be baptized,
no catechumen confirmed, while in the church catechism thousands
are learning and reciting the Apostles' Creed from week to week.
What an influence all this must exert in maintaining sound doctrine and not only doctrine but *unity*. This indeed was the chief
object from the very first of introducing creeds into public worship.

That the Church throughout the world in essentials should believe the same thing. All branches of the earlier Church in drawing their Creeds kept this object in view, making them substantially the same as the Apostles' Creed, although clothed perhaps in other words. This was the model, the root and original of all the ancient Creeds. So long as men were content to differ on other subjects, provided they agreed on these articles of faith, there was no schism; and to restore the unity of the Church now, it is only necessary for men to sacrifice their opinions on minor points, and rally around the Apostles' Creed as a bond of union. Those who agree in this, agree in the main. Their differences did not hinder the multitude from uniting in the rehearsal of the Apostles' Creed in Philadelphia lately. This shows that the Creed not only unites those who are Episcopalians, but is a bond still unsevered between them and orthodox Christians of other names. The idea which the public rehearsal of the Creed is meant to realize, is sublime. It is that of the Church on earth joining, as do the angels in heaven, in honouring and glorifying God, doing homage to Him as their Creator, confessing Him to be their Redeemer and Sanctifier, and proclaiming their indebtedness as sinners, to his grace and Spirit. The value of such an acknowledgment depends indeed upon the sincerity of those who make it; but supposing them to be sincere, the Creed is just such a profession as their zeal for God's glory would prompt them to make. All through our services the Church takes the sincerity of her members for granted, and makes them speak accordingly.

3.) Again, the Creed may be *the means of converting sinners.*— It brings Gospel truths before them in the clearest manner. Does it not remind them of the Saviour whom they neglect, of the God whom they offend, of the tribunal to which they are hurrying?— And may it not lead them to think of the end of their sinful course.

The Reading-desk preaches as well as the Pulpit. After a Church had been gathered in New Zealand, a missionary remarked "that the sacred truths found in our book of Common Prayer had been one of the grand means of the conversion of the natives. When any strangers come into the chapel and hear the Liturgy" he says they exclaim "Ah! those are not native prayers. If we did as those persons pray for us to do, we should be very different from what we are. We should cast away all our sins, we should believe in their God, and be made like them in all their doings." If such be the effect of our service when read in the ears of the heathen, why should it not be the same here? Many hearers in our churches find it easier to understand the prayer book than the preacher. It contains no difficult thoughts; no crabbed words or involved sentences. The poor man to whose untutored mind scholarly language conveys no idea, draws from the Liturgy comfort and instruction. I remember reading that a poor woman who had been attentive to her church, observed when on her death bed, that however excellent might be the preacher, "there was something that the other minister, the gentleman in white, used to read, that did her most good " The truth was, that unable to read herself, the plain saxon of the prayer book was more intelligible to her than the polished words of the pulpit.

III.—The next thing I shall speak of is *the custom of bowing in the Creed at the name of Jesus.* They who conform to this custom do it of their own accord, and very few in our Church do it any where but in this part of the service. Of late however, some have endeavoured to introduce the custom of bowing whenever the Lord's name occurs and when doing so, of turning to "the altar." This is not a Protestant practice. It comes from the Romanists, who, believing that the priest has the power of converting bread into the actual body of Christ, do reverence to the table where it lays. The custom of bowing in the Creed at all, is unauthorized by the American Church; but descending, as we do, from the Church of England, many follow her practice in this particular. It is ordered in her 18th Canon, that "when in time of Divine Service the Lord Jesus shall be mentioned, due and lowly reverence shall be done by all persons present." Very few, however, even of the English, do it excepting in the Creed. Some say that if we do it there, we we might as well bow in all other places where the name of Jesus is mentioned; but here we think a medium between two extremes is preferable. I would not altogether omit such an ancient custom on the one hand, nor carry it too far on the other; because if not in England, yet here, the too frequent use of that gesture is apt to offend, and it is not worth while to excite prejudice against our Liturgy, for the sake of a thing of so little consequence. If it be to show that we adore Christ as God, against the Unitarians, or to show against the Romanists, that it is the Lord himself, not his cross nor his mother whom Protestants worship, or to testify by its outward sign our inward reverence for Jesus, that we bow when his name is mentioned, is it not enough for us to do it in the Creed? If we do it there, may we not well be *understood* to do it every where? We can never do too much to show our respect for Him, but as it would be thought absurd before an earthly sovereign to be *always* rendering him the outward homage customary on entering the presence chamber, so the custom of bowing *whenever* the name of Jesus is mentioned, appears superfluous. If done at all, the Creed, as a formal acknowledgment of our belief in the persons of the Trinity, seems to be the proper place; but since our Church does not prescribe the practice, no man is out of order who omits it; much less are those in order who, because they always bow at the name of Jesus in the Liturgy, find fault with those who do otherwise.

2.) Another difficulty with some people in regard to the Creed refers to the *descent of Christ into hell.* They are shocked at the idea of his going to the very place to save us from which he came into the world; nor can they be induced to open their lips in this Article. This arises from their not knowing that the Creed is translated from another language, and that the translators did not use the word hell in the sense of the place of punishment. Doddridge says in his Commentary, that "to this day in the western counties of England, "to hell" over a thing, is to cover or conceal it;" and as the Greek word "hades" means a "concealed or unseen place," "hell" was really the English word which expressed its meaning. Even in the Bible, when hades signifies the grave, it is translated hell, because the grave is the place where the body is concealed after death. It is said on this account in the rubric prefixed to the Creed, that to say that Christ descended into hell, is the same thing as to say that "he went into the place of departed spirits;" because souls on quitting the body are concealed in the place of departed spirits from our eyes, just as the body after interment is concealed in the grave. It does not follow that because this article was put in the Creed to prove that Christ had a human soul, that his soul went, after it left the body, into the place of punishment; because its going there would be no stronger evidence of his having a human soul, than its going where other disembodied spirits go.—His soul went on the very day he died, where that of the converted thief went, a place concealed from us, which we cannot see; and so we say that he went into the place of departed spirits, or descended into hell; which, as I said before, signified a place of concealment. This is often the meaning of the word translated hell in the Bible.

In the Apocalypse, Christ is represented as saying "I have the keys of death and hades," or the place of departed spirits; and we read in tho same book, "Lo, a pale horse, and his name that sat on him was death, and hades followed with him," where death and the souls in the invisible state are represented as moving in awful procession. Again we are told, that "Death and Hades delivered up the dead which were in them," or that the bodies of men had come from their graves, and their souls from the invisible state at the resurrection. St. Peter also, in the Acts of the Apostles says, when speaking of Christ, that "his soul was not left in Hades, neither his flesh did see corruption;" meaning that his body was not left long enough in the grave to be decomposed, nor his soul permitted to continue in the separate state, since he rose on the third day. In all these places the word hades is translated hell, and in all of them the word hell signifies the place of departed spirits, which sufficiently explains its being said in the rubric that the word hell and the place of departed spirits mean the same thing. The fact is, that the word hell stands as the translation of four different words in the Bible, but like many words in our language, it has come, in the course of time, to be used only in one sense; so that many people ignorant of this circumstance, suppose that wherever they meet with it, it means the place of punishment. When our Lord says "Fear not them who kill the body, but cannot kill the soul; but rather fear him who can destroy both soul and body in hell;" the word in tho original is a very different one from that which is translated hell in the Creed and that used by St. Peter, when he says, "God spared not the angels that sinned; but cast them down to hell," is again different from both of them. In those places undoubtedly, the region of the lost is spoken of, and the misunderstanding has arisen from giving the same rendering to different words, when they were capable of another sense.

3.) Another thing should be noticed. Many suppose that to speak of the *holy Catholic Church*, is to copy the Romanists, who would monopolize that term for their own communion, and who arrogantly assume to themselves the name of Catholics. I have protested before in these lectures against the injustice of condemning us for adopting any thing in common with the Church of Rome. On being blamed for sanctioning the using of hymns to song airs, John Wesley is said to have answered, that he "saw no reason why the Devil should have all the good tunes;" and in like manner wo see no reason why the word Catholic should be exclusively appropriated to the Church of Rome, any more than the anthems and prayers which we borrowed from them; for as Dr. Southey remarks, "the Liturgy of the Church of England, (and of course our own,) was compiled from the different Roman offices used in that kingdom; whatever was unexceptionable was retained, all that savoured of superstition was discarded." But with regard to the title we are speaking of, the Church of Rome might as well say at once, as in fact she does, that none except those of her own Communion, belong to the Church of Christ, as call herself the Catholic Church, for the word Catholic means universal. The Catholic Church consists of the countless host of every nation and kindred and tongue and people, who profess the Christian religion; and as Archbishop Secker says, the Church of Rome is no more the Catholic Church, "than one diseased limb, though perhaps the larger for being diseased, is the whole body of a man."

I need say nothing of the Creed which it is discretionary with the minister to use, in place of the Apostles', because there is only this difference between them, that in the Nicene, so called from the place where the Council met which approved it—there is more stress laid upon the divinity of Christ, and his equality with the Father, than in the other. He is not only called the Son of God, but the Creator, "God of God, of the same substance with the Father;" and this was done against the Arians, who denied it.

And now, nothing remains for us to explain of the Morning Service, but the last of its three divisions. The first is Confession, the second praise, and the third prayer. This shall be our topic on another occasion. I will only observe in conclusion, that we must not only confess the articles of the Creed with our lips, but believe them in our hearts, and act upon them in our lives. It is not a merely intellectual faith that will avail us any thing, but such a strong and lively one as comes from a sense of our need of all the offices of the Holy Trinity, of the gift of the Father, the atonement of the Son, and the sanctification of the Holy Ghost. May we so believe that "being justified by faith, we may have peace with God through our Lord Jesus Christ." Amen.

THE POOR TRADE.

For what shall it profit a man if he shall gain the whole world and lose his own soul? Or what shall a man give in exchange for his soul?

Mark 8: 36, 37.

WE often hear of people making great sacrifices to save their credit. Of two evils they prefer the less; a heavy loss to a failure, a temporary inconvenience to utter ruin. Jesus Christ urges us to act in religion on the same principle. "Whosoever will come after me," he says, must "deny himself, and take up his cross and follow me." But thousands are unwilling to make the sacrifices which this involves. They are too much attached to the world. Our Lord asks them to reflect. He says, "think, think; suppose you have every enjoyment possible in this life, what good will it do you if you are lost in the next? Will your great possessions, he asks, redeem your soul? Will they be taken in exchange for your soul? Better sacrifice something here than lose all hereafter; for, "what shall it profit a man if he shall gain the whole world and lose his own soul, or what shall a man give in exchange for his soul?" There are three things implied here about the soul; its danger, its value, and its salvation.

I.—First then, *the Soul is in danger.* How do I prove that? Does not Christ say that a man may "lose his own soul"? There is the proof. Satan may try to persuade you of the contrary. He may tell you as he did Eve, that God does not mean what He says;

that you need not be alarmed. But Satan is the "Father of lies."
If Satan wrote a commentary on the Bible, he would pluck every
thorn out of it that could pierce the heart. He would make it a
downy bed for the sinner to lie upon until he went to hell. I had
a remarkable proof lately of Satanic comment. A young man told
me the other day that there was no force in the text, because the
word translated "soul," means life. It is nothing more, he said,
than asking what the better off a man would be for possessing the
whole world after the breath left his body? This is a specimen of
Satan's mode of persuading sinners that they are in no danger.—
What need was there of Christ telling us that the possession of the
whole world would be of no use to a man after he was dead? We
know that; and its only effect would be to attach us more strongly
to the world; to make its brief duration a reason for enjoying it
as much as possible. Christ's design was quite the contrary. It
was to persuade us to renounce the world; to deny ourselves, and
take up His cross and follow Him; and the inducement He offers
is not that the world cannot profit us after death, which as I said
before, would be no inducement at all, but that the soul may be lost,
and that in comparison with the loss of the soul, the gain of the
whole world would be nothing. I wonder if He were not thinking
of His own temptation, when Satan took Him up into a high mountain, and showed Him all the kingdoms of the world and the glory
of them, and said unto Him, "All these things will I give thee
if thou wilt fall down and worship me." But I repeat that the
soul is in danger. "Thus saith the Lord, the soul that sinneth,
it shall die." Now is there one here who can lay his hand on his
heart, and say, "I have not sinned"? Not one. Then observe that
this danger is not confined to great sinners. It hangs over every
one that has sinned; mark that. If you have broken one jot or
tittle of the law of God; if you have done so in thought, word or

deed. If you have done one thing which the law forbids, or left undone one thing which it requires, your soul is in danger, for it is written, "the soul that sinneth it shall die."

Again, if the soul is in no danger, *how is it that men in general* think otherwise? The impression that without satisfaction God cannot, consistently with His justice, pardon sin, is universal. Where is the nation in which sacrifices have not been offered, from the conviction that either the sinner must be punished, or sin expiated? No matter how defective their theology in other respects. In this, at least, the heathen were right, that God is just. Those words were graven on their hearts by the same hand that wrote on tables of stone, and made them offer up even " the fruit of their body for the sin of their soul."

Then look at *Conscience*. Conscience is the alarm-bell of the soul. Its harsh, clanking sound warns the soul of its danger, just as the fire-bell warns us that a house is in flames. Call you it a false alarm? Do you suppose then that the cheat in that case would not be discovered by this time? Do you suppose that men in all ages would have submitted to the tormenting fears of Conscience, if there had been no ground for them? I do not believe that Lawgivers and Statesmen invented the doctrine of future punishment to keep men in order. No sham would answer that purpose; it would have been found out and exposed long ago. Conscience is called the moral sense: the sense, that is, that we are the subjects of moral government. It indicates in a tender and enlightened state the slightest deviation from right, more nicely than the most accurate chronometers the true time. It has been known to make people repair in manhood the petty injuries of their youth. It has caused murderers to confess their guilt, and robbers to disgorge their prey, when else discovery had been impossible. The nearer a man is to death, the more clamorous does conscience become, if he is unprepared to die.

> "No ear can hear, no tongue can tell,
> " The tortures of that inward hell."

When John Randolph was on his death-bed, he cried out, " Remorse ! Remorse ! Remorse !" The bell of conscience tolls louder in some hearts than in others, but it is heard in all, and as the danger of the soul increases by the approach of death, so the tones of conscience then are deeper and quicker than before.

But now we come to the *cause of this danger*. The chief cause lies in the soul itself. The soul is full of inbred sin; of what our ninth Article calls " the fault and corruption of every man," and " the infection of nature." "Being by nature born in sin, and the children of wrath" says our Catechism. The children of wrath, because born in sin. There is the danger and its cause. You know that hereditary disease is in the blood and bones. It cannot be got out of the flesh. So with inbred sin ; it comes from Adam. You can no more work it out, or scourge it out, or starve it out, than you could extract by lancets the taint of scrofula. Like the ancient leprosy, it can only be cured by God himself : and unless so cured it will kill the soul at last. It will make the soul as rotten and corrupt as some putrid diseases make the body. The danger may not be apparent. There may be no sign of spiritual death visible in the sinner. He may outwardly appear to great advantage, but as the seeds of disease often lurk in a lovely form, so outward appearances are no criterion of the state of the soul. Look at that caterpillar ; what does it contain ? A butterfly. In time, if nothing happens, it will emerge from the chrysalis radiant with beauty and full of life. The human body contains a soul; in time, if healthy, it will come forth in all the beauty of holiness and disport itself for ever in the garden above. But the caterpillar does not always produce a butterfly. An insect attacks and eats it out. The caterpillar looks well, but the beautiful tenant of its body is the food of worms; so that when the butterfly should appear you see nothing but the caterpillar's "empty skin." In like manner many a man outwardly looks well enough, but there is the canker of inbred sin in his soul, and when the body dies there is no beautiful spirit to fly away to heaven, but only a dead, corrupt, worm-eaten soul to be cast into hell.

Again, *inbred sin gives rise to many actual transgressions, and the soul is in danger from that cause.* How long in any given case God's forbearance with a sinner lasts, we cannot say, but doubtless it has a limit. It ends when a man fills up the measure of his iniquities. God says at length of every barren fig-tree, "Cut it down, why cumbereth it the ground." The soul is in danger every moment of that sentence. It is like a man on the scaffold before the drop falls, or with his head on the block before the axe descends. The fatal blow is ready; the arm is lifted up to strike; nothing is wanting but the word. And can God be provoked to speak it? He can; "He is angry with the wicked every day. If they turn not, He will whet His sword; He hath bent His bow and made it ready." Every day that one abides in sin, and rejects Christ, and persists in wickedness, he dares God, if I may so express myself, to speak that word. Every sin he commits, and every duty he neglects is a challenge to the Almighty to sign the death warrant of his soul. Am I too earnest? Were you ever on board a ship when the cry of "breakers a-head" was heard from the forecastle, or the alarm of fire given, or the sign of a hurricane descried in the heavens? If so, did the captain, or chief officer mince his words? No, they shouted "about ship! all hands on deck!"

as if they had throats of brass and lungs of steel. And would you have me do less when the precious soul is in danger of shipwreck? A man once asked a minister if he believed what he preached? " Certainly I do." " Then why don't you speak as if you did ?" replied the other. Ah! no man ever did much in the pulpit who uttered the most solemn truths as if he did not believe them.— Look at that man on the banks of the Jordan clothed with a rough garment, and leathern girdle. The very stones almost wept when he cried, " repent, for the kingdom of heaven is at hand." Look at Christ asking imploringly, " What shall it profit a man if he shall gain the whole world and lose his own soul ?" The danger of the soul warrants all the earnestness of manner, and all the plainness of speech possible. The soul is in danger from indifference, neglect, and love of ease ; from the temptations of the world, the flesh, and the devil. From formalism, false doctrine, and self-deception. It is as much in danger from little sins as from great ones ; just as a spider's bite may prove as fatal as a rattlesnake's ; and yet how little is thought of them! Thus the danger is increased by being underrated, just as we are in more peril from unsuspected enemies than from open ones. There is danger arising to the soul from so many causes, that as you would watch a ship driving on the rocks, even so I believe do evil spirits watch the progress of every man to ruin. If he escape, they howl; if he perish, they shout like wreckers on the coast. Thank God, he sometimes escapes. I fancy that I see thousands of these, our enemies, recording our sins. Perhaps they know how many we shall be allowed to commit before destruction, and eagerly count them as they pass. They know, at any rate, that every sin brings us nearer to death. Look at one of them. You see that he writes in crimson letters. He has reached the last page. A few more sins, and the volume will be complete. What a sneer of triumph is on his face when he looks downward !

But just as he is inserting the final word, the crimson covered page becomes a blank. Praise God for that! He sometimes takes their prey from their hands at the very moment when they think it sure, and "though his sins be as scarlet they become white as snow, though red like crimson, they are made as wool."

II.—We come now to the second point, *the value of the soul.*— Our Lord says that the whole world would not atone for its loss. I defy any one to compute the value of the soul; but that he who barters it for the world gains no equivalent, is soon demonstrated. For mark, first, that the world is made of *mean materials.* That indeed renders it a more glorious display of God's power, but none but savages prefer glass beads however beautiful, to a string of pearls, or a copper bolt to pure gold. But the soul is not even material. It was not formed out of the dust. It is no common soul like that of the brute. It is a high born and heaven-descended soul, and the marks were stamped on it at first of its divine original. It bore the image of God. It was the mirror of His perfections, and a faithful copy of His moral excellence. What can you say of the world in comparison? Its mountains—what are they but sublime accumulations of dust? Its treasures—what are they but dust in metallic, mineral, or crystallized forms? Its loveliest scenes—what are they but material modifications of grace and beauty? Looking then merely at what they are made of; that the one is material and the other spiritual; "what shall it profit a man if he shall gain the whole world and lose his own soul?"

But besides that the world is *perishable.* We see the proof of that everywhere. The world is full of the remains of things that have once existed. It is replete also with changes. That prairie was once the bed of the sea; this island a part of the main land;

B

those rocks have been severed from the adjoining mountain. The earth is full of subterranean fires. We read that the world and all that it contains shall be burnt up. The whole world is a vast volcano, whereby some day all the works that are therein shall be reduced to ashes. The Soul, on the contrary, is immortal. It will survive "the wreck of elements and crush of worlds."

> "Cold in the dust this perished form may lie,
> But that which warmed it once will never die."

Some, because the soul is invisible, have denied its existence; but they might as well deny the existence of God, "for no man hath seen God at any time." They might as well deny the existence of all the objects that can only be seen by a magnifying-glass, as say that because they cannot see the soul, they have got none. They have puzzled themselves also to find out the precise locality of the soul, whether it resides in the brain or elsewhere, but that is of little moment. The existence of the soul is asserted by the soul itself. There are some places nearer to where it comes from than others; and when we go to such places the soul seems agitated. If unprepared to die, the man feels when in those places that there is a future state. The soul tells him so by groanings that cannot be uttered. Have you known nothing of this when you stood by the bedside of a dying friend, and he slowly turned his languid eyes on you and whispered " good-by"? Or when you took leave of his poor body before they shut on it the door of its narrow house ? Even infidels are not strangers to such feelings.— There was an arch infidel who because of them wished "that he had never been born," and another said "there is one thing that poisons all the pleasures of my life; the thought that the Bible may be true." Ah! the soul is immortal! "It must be so, else," as Addison says,

"Whence this pleasing hope, this fond desire,
This longing after immortality?
Or whence this secret dread and inward horror
Of falling into nought? Why shrinks the Soul
Back on itself, and startles at destruction?
'Tis the divinity that stirs within us!
'Tis heaven itself that points out a hereafter,
And intimates eternity to man."——

God taught the immortality of the soul when He told Moses two hundred years after Jacob's death, that He was the God of Jacob still; "for He is not the God of the dead, but of the living." How many ages had elapsed since the death of Moses and Elias when the disciples saw them alive upon the mountain! Dead men are soon forgotten. The old saying, "out of sight out of mind," is more true of the dead than of the living, but all live unto God. The souls of those who have died these five thousand eight hundred and fifty-seven years, like so many harvests are gathered into his garners, and await only the redemption of the body to enter into hell or heaven. "What shall it profit a man if he shall gain the whole world and lose his own soul." They will not bear comparison; the man who would barter his soul for the world, is sillier than the Indian who gives gems for fish-hooks, and pearls for toys. The folly of doing so has been acknowledged over and over again, by men in dying circumstances. I have read of a merchant who offered his physician a hundred thousand dollars to prolong his life for three days, that he might attend to the concerns of his soul. The truth is, that its immense value looms up before the eyes closing in death, as the land does out of the fog to the approaching mariner. But indeed, we can form no adequate idea of the value of the soul. Its only measure is the precious blood of Christ which was shed for its redemption. All we know about it is this, that if the soul be lost, all its faculties in place of making us happy, will make us miserable; that reason, memory, affection, enjoyment, the favour of God, the companionship of angels, the recognition of friends, the blessedness of heaven, glory, honour and immortality, depend on its salvation. When Societies for the conversion of Jews were first established they were a good deal ridiculed. A mathematician said that "he did not suppose they would convert a hundred altogether." "Be it so," replied a converted Jew, "but take your pen if you please, and calculate the value of a hundred souls."— Well said, child of Abraham! He might as well have tried to count how many atoms there are in the Universe, as to solve that question. Why such is the value of the soul that the conversion of one makes heaven frantic, as it were, with joy. Little that transpires on earth do the angels care for. They take no notice of the triumphs of art and science; but those of grace absorb their interest. When Newton discovered the law that controls worlds, and Galileo the telescope, they paid no attention; but when a stray sheep of Christ is brought home, they make heaven ring with hallelujahs. Our Lord's words imply strongly that there is no comparison between the value of the soul and the world. It is not in doubt He asks "What shall it profit a man if he shall gain the whole world and lose his own soul;" but to make the folly of doing so more conspicuous. For suppose a man did gain the whole world, the net profit to him would be vastly less than the gross amount. A very small portion would satisfy his wants, and what could he do with the surplus? Would he gain any thing by having more wealth than he could spend, more pleasure than he could enjoy, or more magnificence than he could display? If you would see the folly of exchanging the soul for the world, just observe how little the world has done for its owners. Look at Napoleon, for instance, of whom more literally than any other can it be said, that he gained the whole world. Look at his toils and cares, his griefs and anxieties, his exile and captivity. Imagine a man of his boundless ambition shut up for life, like a lion in a cage, on a rock ten miles long and six broad. Buried as it were alive, and not allowed, even when he died, the grave he asked for. Ah! but you say, nineteen years afterwards they bore his ashes triumphantly to France, and consigned them with pomp to a gorgeous sepulchre. True, but what of that?

> "Can storied urn or animated bust
> Back to its mansion call the fleeting breath?
> Can honour's voice provoke the silent dust,
> Or flattery soothe the dull, cold ear of death?"

Look not at his sumptuous funeral; go rather into that tent where they have uncovered his remains. Look at the dead face, the skeleton limbs and the wasted form. They who bend over them look on with breathless interest; but let the prophet tell us their thoughts on reviewing the loathsome spectacle. " They that see thee shall narrowly look upon thee, and consider thee, saying Is this the man that made the earth to tremble, that did shake kingdoms, that made the world as a wilderness and the cities thereof?" Follow that soul into the invisible state. He talked of it just before he died, as the Elysian Fields. He made its chief joy to consist in talking over with his comrades their deeds of arms, but instead of that they only say to him, "art thou also become as weak as we? art thou become like unto us? Thy pomp is brought down to the grave and the noise of thy viols; the worm is spread under thee and the worms cover thee. How art thou fallen from heaven, O Lucifer, son of the morning! How art thou cut down to the ground which didst weaken the nations!" Brethren, there was no end of this man's riches. He had gold, and silver, and gems, and jewels; and houses, and lands innumerable. He was distinguished and renowned. His will was a law which even kings and princes submitted to. The share of the world that may fall to our lot is not to be mentioned in the same breath with his. If the world proved to him so unprofitable, what can we expect from it? "What shall it profit a man if he gain the whole world and lose his own soul?"

III.—I have little time to speak of the third point, unless you will bear with me a little longer. The text implies *that the soul may be saved.*

How can that be? you ask. Wherewith shall we purchase its salvation? The price must be as much as the soul is worth.— We have nothing to give in exchange for the soul. True, but no more has that poor man anything to give for the redemption of his heavily mortgaged lands. But suppose a rich neighbour pays his debts and takes out for him a quit-claim; is it not the same as if he paid them himself? And suppose Christ renders satisfaction to God for our sins, makes himself responsible for them, bears the whole burden of their punishment: if God consents to receive payment in our stead at his hands, are we not relieved from paying them ourselves? Is not God's claim against us as much cancelled as though we had? There is no condemnation to them who are in Christ Jesus. The soul is saved from the guilt of sin by having its guilt transferred to Christ, for "He was wounded for our transgressions, He was bruised for our iniquities, the chastisement of our peace was upon Him, and with His stripes we are healed."

Ah! but you say, there is my sinful nature, what will you do with that? "Without holiness no man shall see the Lord;" and I love sin, I am its slave, and I have tried a thousand times to mend without success. My soul is not fit for heaven in that state. True, but what does God say to that? He says, "I will put my Spirit within you. I will put a new heart within you" I will give you a will and desires and affections like my own. Now does not that

meet the difficulty? If you love what God loves, are you not fit to
live with God? Will you be the slave of sin if Christ puts His
spirit in your heart and causes you to walk in his statutes? No,
" for to whom ye yield yourselves servants to obey, his servants ye
are to whom ye obey." If Christ "shall make you free, ye shall
be free indeed." You remind me, perhaps, of the frailties, and
imperfections, and falls of Christians; but what do they prove?
Only that the old Adam dies hard; only that the flesh lusteth
against the spirit." Is a soldier vanquished because he is wounded,
or a willing slave because he falls into an ambush? No more is a
Christian conquered because he is overtaken by sin, or entangled in
the nets and snares of the devil. If a Christian do wrong, there
comes upon him from the world a storm of ridicule and derision;
but where has Christ promised immunity from sin to his people?
He says, "sin shall not have dominion over you," but He does not
say it shall not strive with you. He does not say it shall trouble
you no longer; he only says it shall be no longer your master. If
I am a child of God, Christ will not only be made unto me "righteousness and redemption," but "sanctification" also. I shall come
off "more than conqueror" at last, although I must expect to be
smitten, and buffeted, and struggled with, until called from the
Christian's conflict on earth, to the peace and pleasures of the
Church in heaven. The soul may be saved then, every provision
has been made for its salvation; but if you would save your soul
you must give up the world. You cannot retain both; one of
them must be surrendered. There are some here, perhaps, who
think they might as well give up life as give up the world, but
they will find as Christ says, that " whosoever will save his life"
in that way "shall lose it." You may enjoy yourselves here no
doubt, for the world has charms; but then it will be said to you
hereafter, " Son, remember that thou in thy lifetime receivedst thy

good things "—You have had your portion, it will be said, That
world in flames was your portion. " Depart into everlasting fire
prepared for the Devil and his angels." I repeat however that the
soul may be saved, and I am the bearer of many invitations from
Jesus Christ to perishing souls; to the weary and heavy laden, to all
who feel sin burdensome, to those who are contrite and broken-
hearted, to the greatest sinners upon earth. Only believe, dear
Brethren; He is able if you are willing. " He is able to save unto
the uttermost all that come unto God by Him."

THE HOLY WAR.

And I will put enmity between thee and the woman, and between thy seed and her seed; it shall bruise thy head, and thou shalt bruise his heel.

Genesis 3 : 15.

WHO can imagine the rage, and disappointment, and wonder of Satan, when he heard these words! They disconcerted all his plans. He thought that he had ruined man beyond redemption. He knew that God could not show mercy at the expense of justice. He knew that without satisfaction to His broken law, He could not let sinners go free; and unable to see where satisfaction could come from, he felt sure of his prey. "I have placed God in a dilemma," he said; "He must destroy the work of his own hands. I have brought Him to such a pinch, and strait, and perplexity, that He has no alternative."

Are you surprised that the possibility of Christ becoming the sinner's surety did not occur to him? Who could suppose that the Father would allow, or the Son consent to such a sacrifice? The thought never entered Satan's mind. God had said unto Adam, "in the day that thou eatest thereof, thou shalt surely die;" and Satan had never known God to postpone punishment; he had no sooner sinned himself than he was cast into hell. He thought therefore, that Adam and Eve would suffer likewise. How amazed he must have been then to hear God say, "I will put enmity between thee and the woman!" There was an end to his hopes of an alliance between men and devils—"And between her seed and thy seed;"

—there was Christ; the first promise of Christ in the Bible, and it demolished Satan's hopes in a moment. He knew what to expect next; the Sinner's reprieve—and sure enough, after God had passed sentence on the serpent, he reprieved his victims. He did not condemn them to die, body and soul, on the very day of their transgression, as He had done at first. They were then under the law, which makes no provision for the sinner's escape; but now they were under the Gospel, which offers sinners, through faith in Christ, a full pardon, and gives them time for repentance. And this accounts, my dear Brethren, for the forbearance and long suffering of God to sinners now. The law condemns them to die at once, and to die eternally; but through the satisfaction of Christ their lives are spared. Unless we neglect the salvation provided in the Gospel, we are in no danger of the eternal death pronounced by the law against sinners; but otherwise the law must infallibly take its course, because there is no Saviour beyond the grave to hinder it. "Now, therefore, is the accepted time; behold, now is the day of salvation." But let us examine the text in detail; I propose to take its parts as they stand, and explain them separately.

I.—"*I will put enmity between thee and the woman.*" It is God Almighty who speaks. None but he can root out the love of sin from the heart, and implant there the love of holiness. God makes us Satan's enemies by converting us into His friends. It needs divine power to accomplish that; "I will put enmity between thee and the woman." It is Eve that is spoken of. Satan had tempted her, not her husband. He gained him over by her influence; and it is still through our affections that he often gains his objects. But it was not chiefly for this, nor because she was the weaker vessel, that he tempted the woman and not the man. It was because by corrupting her he corrupted her children. By poisoning the root of the tree, he poisoned the branches; by polluting the fountain, he defiled the waters. How is it that we are all "by nature the children of wrath?" Because Eve was our mother, and as her offspring we inherit her fallen nature. That was why Satan tempted the woman. In order that by making her a sinner, all her posterity might be sinners too. But God defeated Satan. He put his grace in her heart; he did but drop a few seeds of holiness there, and Eve became Satan's inveterate foe. He cannot boast that he bore away his first victim in triumph to hell. She was snatched by sovereign grace out of his hands. You see that I take it for granted that Eve was saved. The enemy of the Devil is God's friend, and no friend of God is lost. I wonder that the fact of Satan's addressing himself to the woman has not taught us the importance of pious mothers. And yet how many send their daughters to popish seminaries and irreligious schools! This is playing into Satan's hand, because through the mothers he secures the children. Only think of the power of maternal influence! It is felt sometimes after the mother has been years in her grave. The Rev. Mr. Knill tells an affecting story of a man, who after being abroad most of his life, returned home. His mother had been long dead. He arrived at night, and it was in her room that he slept. On awaking he beheld every thing as he had left it in youth.— He beheld the chair she sat in, the books she read, the couch she pressed. He saw the spot where forty years before, she used to say to him, "Come, my dear, kneel down with me, and I will go to prayer." The strong man wept like a child, and falling down on his knees in the same place, he poured forth his heart to God. Oh! seek that God may say of your daughters as He did of Eve, "I will put enmity between thee and the Woman."

Some say that there was no need of God doing this: that enmity between them would be the natural consequence of what had happened. I admit that Eve had no cause to like the Serpent, nor

the Serpent, Eve. The loss of Eden, herself ruined, her husband
betrayed; he condemned to toil, she to sorrow; these wrongs one
would think were quite enough to set the woman against Satan;
and he might well feel spitefully against her as the mother of the
promised Seed. But in fact, the man out of Christ is not be found,
who feels so keenly the injuries inflicted on our race by Satan as to
wage war against him on that account. The enmity spoken of is
one which leads to hostilities, to actual strife. No man will own
to being Satan's friend; but where is the unconverted man who
acts as his enemy, or who is not in some way or other his ally? No;
as some animals are enraged by the sight of certain colours, so is
Satan enraged by the sight of holiness; God changed the heart of
Eve; He opened her eyes to see the deformity of sin; He made her
a holy woman, and Satan was infuriated. Thus it was that God put
enmity between Eve and the Serpent. He hated her for her holiness, she him for his depravity.

II.—I come now to the second part of the text; "*I will put
enmity between thy seed and her seed.*" Not only between Eve
and the Serpent, but between their respective offspring. The
head and members of the one family, should hate the head and
members of the other. Here Eve stands for the Church, and as
Christ is the head of the Church, let us see *how God kept his
promise as far as He is concerned.* He sent the holy child Jesus
into the world. Born of a virgin indeed, but "conceived of the
Holy Ghost." Truly man, but also truly God, and of course having a burning hatred to everything in the shape of sin. In how
many instances did Christ evince this feeling! What did he say to
the Scribes and Pharisees who assailed Him? He said, "Ye serpents! ye generation of vipers, how can ye escape the damnation of
hell? Was that the language of affection? Even when Peter "spake

unadvisedly with his lips"—said something that looked as if the
Devil were concerned in it, our Lord turned on him, as one who
saw a snake might turn on it. He said to Peter, (and the words
sound as if spoken sternly and frowningly,) "Get thee behind me
Satan, thou art an offence unto me, for thou savourest not the things
that be of God, but those that be of men." There is one sense, I
admit in which Christ loves sinners. As "wretched, and miserable,
and poor, and blind" creatures, condemned to eternal death. In
that sense I grant you he loves them, but it is with the love of
pity and compassion, not of complacency or delight. I remember
reading of a poor sawyer, who, when eating his loaf on a wood pile,
seeing a poor starving woman gaze at him, gave her half of it, saying, "Although I ain't rich, I am generous." That was the sort of
affection of Christ for sinners—generous, sympathizing. It brought
tears into his eyes to see us starving for the bread of life, so that
"though he was rich, yet for our sakes he became poor, that we
through his poverty might be rich." But Christ has no fondness,
or partiality, or admiration for sinners. He feels for them repug-
nance, disgust and aversion, as they are opposed to God. If he
loves them as sinners, would he have shed his blood to make them
otherwise? No: his very exertions to give them the opposite character, prove that they are hateful to him in that of sinners. He
loves their immortal souls, he loves them for what they might be,
but not for what they are. We read in Church history, that Gre-
gory 1st, seeing young and noble looking men prisoners at Rome,
on being told that they came from England, said, "These English,
if Christians, would be angels." So I think Christ says of sinners.
He loves them for what they might be. He says if these sinners
were saints, they would be angels. Perhaps you think that no
one will be lost, since Christ died for sinners. Do not trust
to that for salvation. Christ holds sinners, as such, in abhor-

rence; He died not to save them in sin but out of sin, not only to
deliver them from its punishment, but from its power. Oh! remember that unless they repent and believe in Jesus, he will say himself
at last to them, "Depart from me ye cursed into everlasting fire,
prepared for the Devil and his angels."

But now take Satan, the head of *his* family, and say if God has
not put enmity *between him and Christ's seed*, as he did between
Christ's and Satan's. Does he not sanctify believers by his Spirit?
Does he not put into their hearts, a hatred of sin, and excite them
to engage in its overthrow? Thus Satan is enraged against them
as reflecting God's image. He beholds in them, as in a glass, that
hated image of holiness, and he flies at and strives to destroy it, as
he flew at our first parents, when in all the beauty and sanctity of
innocence they dwelt in Eden. See how he afflicted Job; how he
buffeted the Apostle Paul; how he smote David, and how he
assailed Peter. Look at the proofs of his rage as you find them in
the annals of Smithfield, of the Inquisition, of the Waldenses, and
of the Huguenots. The rage of Satan against the people of God
is exasperated *by their zealous and successful labours*. I ascribe the
insurrection now going on in British India almost entirely to this
circumstance. English and American Christians have for many
years been labouring there to convert the heathen. For a long
time Satan seemed to regard their efforts as beneath his notice. But
showers of blessing descended upon the Indian missions. The pulpit and the press in Bengal especially were made powerful to pull
down the strong holds of Satan. Whole villages were converted at
once. Hundreds renounced their caste, and threw away their idols
to the moles and to the bats. The Suttee was abolished, and the
power of Christianity began to be felt. And what did Satan do
then? He went to the Brahmin as he sat with the seal of his caste
upon his brow in the temple, and said to him, unless you destroy

the Christians, they will subvert your influence and break down your altars. And then he went to the Mahometan, and said unless you destroy the Christians, the cross will supplant the crescent. And to all the superstitious soldiery he said, Fight for your gods. Then they rose in mass, putting Christians to the sword, and subjecting native converts to the most barbarous tortures. It is idle to say that religion had no concern in the movement. India has been far happier under British rule than it ever was under that of its native princes; and whatever political causes may have aided the insurrection, the hostility of Satan to the woman's seed underlays them all. Never have savages been guilty of such cruelties as those to which the slaves of Satan in India were instigated on this occasion. There is but one gleam of comfort to be drawn from it, namely, that if there were not many Davids in the camp of Israel, the champion of the Philistines would be less wrathy and vindictive.

But from the heads of these families *turn to their children.*— Between good and bad men there has always been enmity. Why did Cain kill Abel? For the strange reason that he was a better man than himself. " Because his own deeds were evil and his brother's righteous." On the same principle, Cain, were he living would not leave a good man on earth. True, and if they had the power, the wicked would destroy the seed of the woman. They would cry out against them as that arch infidel Voltaire did against Christ himself, " Ecrasez l'infame," crush the wretch. Cain and Abel are not the only persons who have been allied by blood, but foes by grace. Parents and children, husbands and wives, brothers and sisters in all ages, have been set at variance by God putting his grace in a household. Many a couple have parted on this account. Many a father has driven a godly son from his door. And what as a class have the wicked done against the righteous? Have they

B

not hunted them with dogs, flayed them alive, burnt them to death, and tortured them in every way they could think of? And what are they doing now? The ministers, and the institutions, and sincere professors of religion are as much hated and abhorred by the wicked now as ever they were. They have not the power to treat Christians now as they did of old; but they scoff and jeer at them.— They exclaim, Away with the Sabbath; make it a day of sports, shut up the churches, turn out the clergy. They hiss and spit venom on their foes like serpents.

And how do good men show their enmity to the wicked? By opposition. They do all they can to hinder the growth of sin in the world, and to convert sinners. Look at those twelve warriors of Christ. They go and plant his standard everywhere. They are "unlearned and ignorant," but no matter, foolish as they are, God makes them able to confound the wise. On the day of Pentecost a single sermon caused three thousand of the enemy to lay down their arms. Their enmity was slain and they came over in a body to the camp of Christ. On the Apostles went, some in one direction and some in another, against the foe. At Antioch, and Athens, and Rome, and Ephesus, they preached the Gospel, and taught the people. No one could say aught against them; their lives agreed with their doctrines, and they did as much harm to the enemy by their practice as by their preaching. Their patience in suffering, their self-denial, their zeal, their holiness conquered thousands through the grace of God. The same contest has been going on ever since the Apostle's days. Every Christian in his family, among his acquaintance, and fellow-citizens, brings all his influence, and example, and means, and abilities, to bear against wickedness and the wicked. To repress the one, and to convert the other, is the aim and end of all the combinations in the Church. Our Sunday Schools, our Missions, our Bible Societies, our Tract Associations, have all sprung from the enmity sown by grace in the seed of the woman, against that of the serpent. It is in fact, the love of souls, and Oh! what zealous and self-denying labours it has produced in Christians! A Bishop of our own church was converted by a negro. He sent for the man, as the Philistines sent for Sampson, to make sport for them at a feast. "Preach for us," he said. The poor man hesitated, but at length, constrained by holy zeal, he spake such solemn truths to the company that many were impressed, and the merry-maker himself was converted to God. The celebrated Mr. Whitfield, such was his zeal, preached eighteen thousand sermons in thirty-four years, to the great discomfiture of Satan Ah! those who feel enmity against the serpent's seed, do something to show it! A parish that does little or nothing for the spread of the Gospel, is like a regiment asleep on the field of battle. No zealous officer would wish to command such a regiment as that.— Being asked to a parish, a clergyman before accepting the call enquired, "What do you do for Foreign Missions?" "Nothing," was the answer. "For Domestic ones then?" "Nothing." "For the Bible Society?" "Nothing." To every question he got the same answer, nothing. Of course he said, "I cannot stay with such a congregation." Nor would he have done so had not the people subscribed three thousand dollars on the spot for these objects. Brethren, if we are the soldiers of Christ we shall fight the devil.

But again, this enmity is displayed not only in the world, but in the heart of the Believer. There is a continual struggle going on there between grace and corruption. We allude to that in the baptismal service where we say, "O merciful God, grant that the old Adam in this child may be so buried that the new man may be raised up in him." I want no stronger proof that God does not put a new heart in every child at baptism than that so few children display after they are baptized any enmity against sin and Satan. The very tendency and workings of grace in the Believer urge him to mortify his sinful affections; and although in his conflict with the old Adam, he too often fails; still by the grace of God he perseveres. Like the Apostle Paul, he feels that the flesh lusteth against the Spirit, and the Spirit against the flesh," but he fights on though in much weakness, and with many infirmities, and God gives him "power and strength to have victory at last," and to "triumph against the world, the flesh, and the devil."

III. — This brings us to the *result of the battle.* "I will put enmity between thee and the woman, and between thy seed and her seed, *it shall bruise thy head, and thou shalt bruise his heel.*" Mark the difference; Satan's head and Christ's heel. The fangs of the serpent are in its head; crush that, and its power to do mischief is gone. The head is a vital part, but the heel is not.— Suppose, that in stamping on a serpent's head, your heel were bruised, it would not amount to a fatal injury. It is not said that the serpent bites the heel, for then it would be poisoned, but only bruises it. The heel, as the lower part of the body, stands for Christ's lower nature, his humanity. The devil was to strike him there; his higher nature, which was divine, he could not touch. Everything that belonged to the nature that had sinned—the nature that Christ had assumed as the sinner's surety, Satan might do his worst with, but there he must stop.

Let us notice two or three points wherein the Serpent bruised Christ's heel.

First by his *temptations.* Here I am at a loss to express myself. What can a sinner tell of the feelings of a pure and undefiled soul? The Devil came to the holy child Jesus in the wilderness and whispered blasphemies. He strove to make him sin against God. Forty days incessantly was He tempted of Satan, who left nothing untried that infernal cunning could think of to make him fall. The pangs of hunger and other physical privations that Christ suffered were nothing to this. You know that Christ is so pure that angels cannot look at him without shading their eyes. And the purer any one is the more exquisitely alive is he to the approach of sin. Oh! then, if the "soul of righteous Lot were vexed with the filthy conversation of the wicked." If good men turn away with disgust from the profane talk of the ungodly—then to be solicited day after day by Satan, to have his fetid breath polluting the very air he breathed, to have the great foe of God and man pouring into his ear vile proposals, must have been a torture to Christ's unsullied soul, beyond our power to imagine.

Satan in another way bruised Christ's heel—*By persecution.*—He never ceased persecuting him from the manger to the grave. Had not God interfered, Satan would have killed Jesus almost as soon as he was born. The Serpent would have choked him in his cradle. He made him as it was an exile, a fugitive. He stirred up all his brood to hiss and slander him. They called him wine-bibber, —glutton,—the boon companion of publicans and sinners. They misrepresented his words, and sent men to play the hypocrite, and lay traps for him. Oh! what a hard life Satan led Jesus! He made the people of Bethlehem turn his parents away.—"There is no room here," they said, "for such as you.—The stall of an ox, and the fodder of cattle are good enough — carry yourselves and your child to the cow stable." He came one day tired, with his disciples, to a village, and Satan so set the villagers against him that they sent him off, they would not so much as give him a bed to lie upon. He himself, in fact says that he was commonly worse off, as far as home and its comforts are concerned, than birds and foxes.

And when Satan found that he could neither bribe, nor tempt, nor force, Christ to serve him, he bound him on a cross of fire and called serpents of hell and earth to see him die. As savages surround their victim, after putting splinters of pine wood into his body and kindling them; so, after driving nails into Christ, Satan and his crew surrounded the cross—The Serpent and his Seed, Christ and his Seed were there. The former yelled and shouted like Indians after scalping their foes. The others, except Christ himself, who "was dumb and opened not his mouth," wept as if their hearts would break to see him suffer. That was the way in which the Devil bruised Christ's heel. He corrupted one of his disciples, and scared the rest. He made one of them deny, and "they all forsook him and fled." He struck a sword through his dear mother before his face. He made him to be a man of sorrows, rejected, reviled, and crucified. You cannot mention a part of the humanity of Christ which Satan did not wound. His heart in its afflictions—his soul in its abhorrence of sin—and his body in all capabilities of suffering. But after all he did no more than "bruise the heel of the seed of the woman," By beating the Serpent's head with his heel, Christ's heel was bruised. His sufferings and death therefore were the means of crushing his enemy. Every blow on his heel was only the recoil of one more fatal on the head of the serpent. "It shall bruise thy head." Even in this life he made Satan feel the loss of power. He converted Sinners.— Satan saw them shedding tears of contrition, and refusing to serve him any longer. He likewise saw his wicked angels cast out. Christ would not permit them to vex the bodies of men as they had done. He drove them to their own place, and made them cry out, "Art thou come to torment us before the time?" Even Death, Satan's jailor, proved faithless when Christ commanded him, for at his order he released his prisoners. All these things were so many blows to Satan, but the crushing blow was still future. The devils shouted, as I said, at the death of Christ, but their joy was of short duration. On the third day he rose again. He seized the keys of the grave out of death's hands, and came forth. That crushed Satan's head virtually for ever, for it secured the redemption of the Church and her seed, and the ultimate damnation of the Serpent and his seed.

And, my dear Brethren, the same glorious issue which crowned the conflict between Christ and Satan will result from that which is going on between his people and their adversary. Satan does bruise their heel. He gains many an advantage through their unfaithfulness, and cowardice, and infirmities. He leads many to sin, he puts many asleep. But they will come off for all that "more than conquerors through Him that loved them." They mortify and bring their bodies and spirits into subjection to the law of Christ. If they fall, they rise again, and renew their attacks on the hateful enemy. They die—their heel is bruised, and their mortal part is committed to the tomb. But when Christ, "who is their life shall appear," by the power of his resurrection, they shall come forth, and joining the host of Angels and Saints attending the glorious Saviour, they shall raise with one accord the victor's song "O Death! where is thy sting! O grave, where is thy victory?"

To conclude: let us see on which side we are ranged in the great battle which is going on between Christ and Satan. Has God put enmity in our hearts against Satan or not? It is not are we kind, and charitable, and free from vice. It is, do we mourn over sin in ourselves and others, and in dependence on divine strength contend against it? Then we are safe, Christ has fought and conquered in our stead all our enemies; and we, through Him, shall be more than conquerors. But if not—if our sympathies are with sin and Satan, their doom must eventually be ours—they will be cast, and all their abettors will be cast into hell. Such will be the end of God's opponents. May sovereign grace slay the natural enmity of our hearts to Him for Christ's sake.—Amen.

THE LABORER'S REST.

―――――――◆・◆―――――――

"Come unto me all ye that labor, and are heavy laden, and I will give you rest."—MATT. xi : 28.

SOME give to these words a very limited application; they confine their meaning to those who *feel* themselves in this state, but, in my opinion, they are addressed to all mankind, because they describe what is the natural condition of all of us. Where is the man who does not labor for something, and who has not a burden of some kind to groan under? If you have ever seen a bark deeply laden, and laboring in the sea, making no headway, but pitching and roliing on the boisterous waves; you have seen the very image here referred to, and there is not a child of Adam to whom it is not more or less applicable. Let us ask then, For what is it that men are laboring? Some for one thing, Brethren, and some for another, although few enough for " the one thing needful." Every man has an object in his eye, the possession of which he believes will make him happy, but what it is depends on circumstances. Do you ask how it is that a diversity of opinion exists upon the nature of happiness? I answer that the soul is like a stray child, seeking but unable to find its home; knowing that it has a home, but alas! not knowing where it is; running in search of it, first in one direction, and then in another, but never finding it until its own Father brings it home in safety.

Some labor for *power*. See how full of fears they are lest they should give offence, and how tremblingly alive to what is said of them! There

is no servitude harder than theirs. They are obliged to stand, like Absalom, at the gate of the city and bow to every one that passes by; to
smile, when their heart is full of grief; to profess what they do not feel;
to flatter fools; to feign virtue; and sometimes even to counterfeit vice.
Nor are their labors over when they grasp their object, for power is even
harder to keep than it is to reach. Few gain its slippery summit, but
fewer still can maintain their footing. It is easier to climb "young ambition's ladder," than it is, when once you "attain the utmost round," to
stay there. Look at the men whose great works and gallant actions
History speaks of. How many of them fell from their giddy eminence!
The most successful aspirant for power that ever lived was bound, like
Prometheus, to a rock, for disease and care to prey upon his vitals.
Some have destroyed themselves; the axe has slain some, and a broken
heart others. And yet how hard they labored in the paths of glory!
They were always revolving schemes, or framing laws, or negociating, or
marching, or fighting, or cultivating the arts of peace. Their bow was
always bent, they neither slept on velvet, nor fed on dainties. They
were men of business, not of pleasure. They worked like galley-slaves
to obtain power, and to keep it, but they had no *rest;* they were on a
treadmill, where to stop was ruin; they dreamed that repose could dwell
with ambition, but they found that to relax the labors for a moment was
to give the signal for their own destruction.

Some men labor for *knowledge,* of which Solomon says, that "of
making many books there is no end, and much study is a weariness of
the flesh." Methinks I see the Apostles of learning in their caves, the
monks in their cloisters, brave old Galileo in his tower, the martyrs of
Science in their dungeons. To such men, who were the hardy pioneers
of useful knowledge, we owe much. I see them with wasted frames and
pale faces, poring over books till daylight. I look on them and upon the
constellations of genius, which, since they have died, have blazed above
our heads. They tell me that the ways of learning are steep and diffi-

cult, that they found themselves, after years of travel, apparently as far from the top as ever; that hill rose above hill, peak above peak, until they wept for vexation. One of them, who measured the stars, and dissected the light, and weighed the earth, says that he picked up a few pebbles from the beach of knowledge, but left the ocean itself unexplored. Some of these men were persecuted, imprisoned, and poor; some were burnt as magicians; many of them died in gaols, garrets and cellars; they were literary hacks and drudges; but they never found *rest* in the pursuit of knowledge; on the contrary, they found, as Solomon says, that "in much wisdom is much grief, and he that increaseth knowledge increaseth sorrow." They found as Kirke White says, that

"For him awaits no balmy sleep,
   He wakes all night, and wakes to weep;
Or by his lonely lamp he sits
   At solemn midnight, when the Peasant sleeps,
In feverish study, and in moody fits,
   His mournful vigils keeps."

Some labor for *wealth*. The stories of the nineteenth century, especially those of gold hunters, will be read as eagerly hereafter, as those about the Philosopher's stone are now. People will say, prodigious! prodigious! to every one of them. You cannot tell what men will do for money, when all they earn is barely enough to keep them alive; but excite their cupidity by the hope of riches, tell them that you have found a land of gold, and you throw the whole world in an uproar. Peter the Hermit's voice, in the eleventh century, had not half the effect upon mankind that the word *gold* had in the year 1849. They sprang as one man, like the high-bred racer that feels the spur, when that talisman was spoken. An Exodus began towards the promised land, far more numerous than that from Egypt; an Exodus from all lands. They covered the earth, as herds of migrating buffalo the prairies. They defied the storms of the Southern Cape, the rugged passes of the Rocky mountains, the fatigues and perils of their dreary march. The eagle, startled at such invasion of his dominions paused. The death of many on the road did not deter their comrades from pressing forward, only to meet on their arrival with greater hardships. And yet all this enthusiasm with regard to most of them, was thrown away. Alas! how few comparatively of those who set out ever returned, and how small a number, even of these, returned rich! But where is the spot on earth so diminutive, or the community so small, as not to furnish proof that men labor hard for the bread which perishes? I can point to towns without churches, to lands without Bibles, to countries without ministers, to districts without schools, and to millions without Christ; but I should be at a loss to look for a place where men are not working, as though their salvation depended on it, to get money. And yet with all their labor they are not satisfied. The "Leech" that "has two daughters" perpetually crying, "give, give," must have a wretched life of it. The man whose avarice is ever tasking him, is like a slave with a driver at his back; if he stops work, down comes the lash; if he complains, the descending whip again urges him. We ought to pity the *poor* man, because he does not labor for money, but bread. Necessity is his task-master, not avarice. When he brings home his wages, his wife says to him—"this will not much more than pay the baker's bill;" but the rich labor for superfluities. Oh! ye rich men, if ye worked less for yourselves, and more for the widow and fatherless, the poor and needy, ye would find more satisfaction in riches. The wise man says that "the abundance of the rich will not suffer him to sleep," his brain is so full of profit and loss, plans and projects, that even when his head is pillowed he cannot rest. The poor man may thank God that he is exempt from, at least, this disquietude. I have seen a poor creature without bed, carpet, chair, or fuel in her room, happier far than some worth thousands. She had nothing on her mind, no investments to make, no houses or land to look after, and above all, contentment in her heart. She could lay her work down, and clasping her hands, look up to heaven, and say, "The Lord is my Shepherd, I shall not want." Our Saviour tells us that "a man's life consisteth not in the abundance of the things that he possesseth"—no indeed, nor his *rest* either. "Come unto me, all ye that labor and are heavy laden, and I will give you rest."

II. Consider in the second place what burdens men carry. And *first*, all who are still in their sins carry a burden of *guilt*. When a man is insolvent, when he owes more than he owns, he is like what, as sinners, we all are toward God; we are bankrupts, burdened with debt; for sin is a debt we owe to God. Every sin is a promissory note, which God holds against us for as much punishment as that sin deserves. When we are told then of God, that he will "by no means clear the guilty," we ought to tremble, for if He do not cancel these notes, we must take them up some day ourselves, brethren. The amount of one of them is large enough to imprison us for ever and ever. We cannot redeem one of those obligations, and all of them will some day be presented for payment. If you were to convert each drop of the sea into a world, and each grain of sand that is on the sea-shore into a mountain, and each blade of grass into a continent, and place the sinner under it, the weight would be nothing compared with the burden of guilt. I see angels laden with it, how acquired I cannot say, but it is round their necks, and it sinks them in a moment down to hell. I see Jesus, as the Surety of sinners, laboring under that load, and his groans and bloody sweat attest its pressure. Many of you are not aware of this burden, because unbelief takes the weight of it from your shoulders. You see a man very attentive in church, you think him very pious, of course; you hear him say, "Lord have mercy upon us, miserable sinners." Well, it is easier to say than to feel that we are miserable sinners; you may see the same man to-morrow evening looking anything but miserable in the dress boxes of the theatre. He does not feel that he is a sinner, he only says so. I repeat that unbelief is the great hindrance to our being sensible of our sins. A porter does not feel his load, though still on his back, whilst something underneath supports it. He who draws water from a well does not feel the weight until the bucket is above the surface; so, until the prop of unbelief is stricken from under him, the sinner does not feel the burden of his guilt. This may be illustrated by an anecdote. A man who was converted under the preaching of Whitfield, confessed that he went to hear him with his pocket full of stones, that he intended to throw at the preacher; "but," said he, "God took away the stone from my heart, and the other stone soon fell from my hand." Unbelief was the stone he referred to. A man will carry the burden of guilt for years, as he did, without it giving him any concern; but as soon as his unbelief is taken away, he cries out in earnest, "God have mercy on me a sinner;" he asks in earnest, "What must I do to be saved?" He no longer speaks of sin as a joke; he is ashamed of it. Look at Adam, skulking away under the sense of it from his Maker's presence; hear Abraham saying in humiliation for it, "I am dust and ashes;" and Job exclaiming, "I am vile." Do not suppose, sinner, that thy portion of guilt is light because thou dost not feel it burdensome. I believe that until the arrows of conviction strike him, a man may have his conscience full of guilt without feeling it; just as a ship might be loaded to the water's edge, but as a few pounds more of freight might send the ship to the bottom, so a few more sins might sink the sinner in perdition. There is such a thing as the cup of a man's iniquity being *full*, one drop more may cause it to overflow, and then, if not before, thou wilt feel thy burden;—when hung like a millstone about thy neck, it is dragging thee downwards, thou wilt ask in vain, "Where shall rest be found?"

> " Ye sinners seek *his grace,*
>   Whose *wrath* ye cannot bear;
> Fly to the shelter of his cross,
>   And find salvation there."

There be many who have a burden of *fears about their soul*. One of the most distressing sights we could look upon, were it revealed to us, would be the secret anxieties that agitate the minds of mortals on this subject. Oh, my brethren, when we turn over the pages of history, and see them marked with the proofs of this, blistered with the tears and stained with the blood that men have shed under the pressure of this burden, what sorrow it begets in the mind! There is the Monk scourging himself, crawling on hands and knees for miles on flint stones. There is the Hindoo swinging on hooks, or lying down to be crushed by the wheels of Juggernaut. There are the priests of Baal, with knives gory with their own blood, and the slaves of Moloch offering "the fruit of their body for the sin of their soul." Such is the anxiety of men about their souls, that they have left all that they had to be laid out in saying masses for their salvation. They have founded hospitals, built churches, enriched shrines, and covered the images of saints with jewels. The Pope took advantage of the fears of men about their souls, to raise funds for the erection of St. Peter's at Rome. They bought his paper for the forgiveness of their sins; they gave good money for his counterfeit notes. Goaded by their fears, men will stoop to anything, and make any sacrifices whereby the least hope is held out to them of finding rest. And yet the load of sin sticks to them; they cannot get rid of their burden of guilt, and so they cannot throw off their burden of fears. There may be dreary and unwelcome thoughts that steal over us at times from this cause—what the Scriptures call "a fearful looking for of judgment." Have you never experienced it, sinner? Have you never, when alone at dusk, with your hands upon your brow, and your eyes fastened on the embers, heard a voice saying unto you, "Thou art not at peace with God, the burden of thy guilt is not removed, thou art still unpardoned, thou art nearing the tomb, take heed lest thou die thus. Escape for thy life?" You felt such thoughts burdensome, and sternly bade them to be gone; but oh, my friend, they are good angels, and always weep as they depart.

A *body of sin*, too, is a burden, and there is no man free from it. Oh, sinner, thou dost make light of this burden; thy names for sins imply that they are mere spots on the sun, nothing but flaws, and that human nature is sound and unfallen. Thou dost call thy sins, not the eruptions of a diseased body, but foibles and misfortunes, like stains, accidentally contracted, and easily removed. But how is it, then, that sin is a universal malady, and that if you cure it in one place, it breaks out in another? I have heard that children are innocent, but if you cross these innocents they are more apt to rebel than to yield. How is it that "a child left to himself bringeth his mother to shame?" Because unaccustomed to control, his corruption, like a wild horse, takes the bit in its mouth and runs away with him. Many a mother has on this account been parted from a child under awful circumstances; she has said "farewell" to him in the prison which he was never to leave, or only leave it to die, because she took no pains to keep under in childhood the propensities and passions of his sinful nature. Let them say what they please, men of the world prove conclusively that they know they carry about with them a body of sin, for they are careful not to show its cloven foot. They swallow the oath that rises trippingly to their tongue. They suppress the anger that contracts their lips; they conceal the malice lurking in their breasts. A young man is apt, like the son of Philip, to ride a horse which every one else is afraid of, but men of the world are more cautious. They may deny that we have a fallen nature, but they feel it pawing and struggling in their hearts, and they hold it in for fear of consequences. Ah, brethren, if we could get rid of this, the tree of guilt would be rooted up, the very spring from which all the streams flow would be dry.

III. Once more, To what sort of rest are we here invited? To one that corresponds with our burdens, brethren. Are you heavy laden with guilt—then Jesus Christ offers to take it away, to pay all your debts to God's justice. They may be in number like the leaves of the trees—they may be in magnitude like the towering Alps—they may be in turpitude of crimson dye—but He says, "Come unto me," and "though your sins be as scarlet, they shall be as white as snow; though they be red like crimson, they shall be as wool." Many a man on paying off his creditors has said, "Thank God, I owe nothing! Thank God, I have that off my mind! What a relief it is that I am out of debt!" But oh, sirs, to have our accounts with God settled, to have one drop of Christ's precious blood fall upon the charges against us in his book, and wash them out forever—this is what sets the mind at ease. Never has a man such a joyful heart as when he is relieved from the burden of guilt. All his *fears* are dispelled, he is not smitten, as he used to be, with misgivings and forebodings on account of sin. His conscience is quieted. Ah, brethren, great is the misery of a disturbed conscience; it stings like an adder; it makes our pleasures like Cleopatra's basket of fruit—an asp is coiled in them; and nothing can quiet it but the blood of Christ. No physician but He can prescribe for that malady. I once read of a celebrated comic actor in Paris who, being subject to fits of melancholy, asked his doctor how to cure them. "Go and see Carline act," was the answer; "if he does not cure you nothing can." A great deal he knew of the matter. "Sir," said his patient, "I am Carline, and while I supply all Paris with mirth, I am myself devoured with melancholy." Ah, thus is it often with sinners, whilst their faces shine like the sun, their hearts are gloomy as midnight. But when a sinner comes to Christ, all the guilt that made his conscience troublesome is transferred to Christ, and Christ's righteousness is transferred to the sinner, so that he has no cause for fear. It is chased away by the sense of pardon, and by the consciousness that "there is no condemnation to them who are in Christ Jesus." He is at rest. He is the Barrabas chosen by Christ, and when he sees the meek and lowly Jesus, bending under the weight of the cross and covered with bleeding wounds, and hears him say, "Sinner, thou art free, I am suffering, and to suffer in thy stead;" although he weeps like a child, and embraces his benefactor's feet, bathing them with his tears, still he feels as if a mountain was taken off his shoulders, and a peace breathed into his heart, "which the world can neither give nor take away."

Again, if you are heavy laden with the burden of your corruptions, Christ offers you rest from the *dominion of sin.* Many are so much the slaves of unruly appetites and passions, that they cannot help giving way to them. They feel themselves degraded, mortified, and make many ineffectual efforts to free themselves, they weep after every indulgence, and curse their folly; but they can no more restrain their passions, than Mazeppa could curb the wild horse they bound him on. What tragedies arising hence do we read of in the daily papers! The glittering knife unsheathed and buried in the heart of the unoffending traveller; the unsuspecting husband murdered by his treacherous companion; the simple girl ruined by the arts of the crafty profligate. No reason we are told can be assigned for half the suicides that happen, but beyond a doubt many destroy themselves because they are the slaves of dangerous and disgraceful habits; they cannot break them, and rather than be trampled under foot by them, or shut up in a prison, or brought to the gallows, they put a pistol to their head and blow their brains out. And can Christ give us rest from this burden? Can He enable me to conquer my passions, to subdue my tempers, and to deny my appetites? Can He enable me to say no to the Tempter, and firmly to resist his motions? Yes, He both can and will put into the hearts of those that come to him, such a hatred of sin and love of holiness as will result in this. They will not go along with their corruptions as a friend, but they will contend with them as an enemy. They will no longer be the slaves and subjects, but the inveterate foes of their corruptions; they will no longer tamely submit to the commands of tyrants, but they will "crucify the flesh with its affections and lusts," and though they struggle and strive to regain the mastery, still through grace preventing they are never able to regain the throne of the heart that is given to Christ.

Once more, and I have done. If you are burdened with a load of *unsatisfied desires*, Christ will give you the rest of *contentment*. He will bring you home to God, sinner. Let the ox seek his food in the meadow, and the lion his prey in the forest, and the hawk its quarry in the sedges; but let the soul seek her satisfaction from God. She is of too high and exalted a nature to be contented with less than God, and she pines because when she doth ask thee for bread, thou dost give her a stone; for the rose might as well seek to grow on the glacier, or the leviathan look for food on the dry land, as the soul find satisfaction in earthly things. God is the proper home of the soul—God breathed the soul, and therefore it is only in union with God that the soul can be happy. Away from God the sinner resembles the ship which our navigators met with floating about in the Arctic seas—he is the sport of the winds and waves—his desires impel him in one direction to-day and in another to-morrow, but he cannot find rest. Jesus offers him rest by restoring him to his place in the universe, his proper place, the favor and enjoyment of his Father in heaven. There the vast capacities of his soul will find adequate and suitable nourishment. It will be filled in the fullness of God, which is inexhaustible. The mind contented, will cease its restlessness. The soul filled with joy and peace in believing, will disdain those objects in which once it placed its chief good, and the whole man will exclaim with David, "Whom have I in heaven but thee, and there is none upon earth that I desire besides thee."

I close, then, with the invitation of the text, "Come to Jesus" for rest. Let those who have not found it in the profits and pleasures of the world, come. Let those who are alarmed lest they should die unpardoned, come. Let those who seek that rest in ordinances which only Christ can give, whose religion is made up of Saints' days, and altars, and prayers, and sacraments, come. Let those come who, although they give half their goods to feed the poor, are still restless because they fall too far short of what the law demands to feel safe. Let the heavy laden with guilt and corruptions, come; nay, "whosoever will let him come and take of the water of life freely."

> " Lord, then whither shall we go,
>   Save to thee, our refuge sure?
> Balm to each bereaving wo,
>   Who alone the heart canst cure;
> Turning sickness into health,
> And to want becoming wealth.

> " Pardon, peace, and purity—
>   Gifts without, and grace within,
> Love and light, which set us free
>   From the curse and chain of sin;
> These, Emanuel, thou canst give,
> While upon thy words we live."

THE HIDING PLACE.

"And a man shall be as an hiding place from the wind, and a covert from the tempest."—ISAIAH xxxii: 2.

THESE words refer in the first place to Hezekiah, King of Judah. When the Assyrians threatened to beseige Jerusalem, and to carry away his people captive, he became their "hiding place," that is, he was the means of their safety, because, in answer to his prayers God in a single night destroyed their enemies. But it is to Jesus Christ, that the text chiefly refers. He shields his people from far greater perils than those which menaced the Jewish monarchy, and he does so by his own arm, not by that of another. He does not ask any one else to deliver them from the coming tempest, but he interposes and suffers the storm to expend all its fury on his own head.

I shall notice, first of all, the *nature*, and secondly, the *offices of Christ*, as they are here presented to us. But before I begin, allow me to say that although the text speaks of Christ as a man, it insinuates that he is much more, because, otherwise, there would be nothing so very wonderful in the Prophet's statement. If all he meant to so say, was that a mere man should deliver his country from danger, he might have said the same thing of Washington, or of any Liberator; but if you understand him to mean that God was "manifest in the flesh," in order to save his people from perils which no mere man could avert, it is indeed a wonder that a man should be "as an hiding place from the wind, and a covert from the tempest."

I. First, then, beloved, with this reserve, we are told that Christ is a man.

Ask some persons why he became a man, and they will tell you that he came to be a model man. That is partly correct, but was there no higher reason than that for his becoming man? See what the Bible says upon that subject: "This is a faithful saying, and worthy of all acceptation, that Christ Jesus came into the world to save sinners." Ah! that accounts, satisfactorily, for his becoming man. He could not have saved sinners by his example. If he had come only to be a model man; if he had come only for sinners to copy, nobody would have been saved, for who could have been his copyists? You might as well expect a man without any love of art, to copy the sublime conceptions of Michael Angelo, as a man without holiness to imitate the purity and perfection of Jesus Christ. He became man, because, to save sinners, it was necessary that he should "put away sin by the sacrifice of himself." That he should some day come into the world for that purpose was taught by the custom of offering sacrifices which at one time or another has prevailed in all countries. You know that human victims were always esteemed to have the most efficacy. How many children among the Assyrians, Phenicians and Carthagenians, perished by this persuasion; Parents cast their little ones into the flaming hands of Saturn, without a tear. Then if you go back to Eden, and mark the coats of skins which clothed our first parents after the fall; and if you go back to Cain, and see him repulsed for bringing fruits, instead of the blood of a lamb, to the altar, and if you go back to Abraham, stretching forth his hand to slay his son; you will see it was all along signified to the world that "without shedding of blood, there is no remission," and that "in the fulness of time, God would send his Son, made of a woman," to "put away sin, by the sacrifice of himself." This was the reason of his becoming man. Had He come as our substitute in any other form, it might have been said to him, "thou art not a man! thou hast no blood to shed. The crimson die of sin can be expunged only by blood drawn from human veins. By man hath the law been dishonored, and by man must it be magnified, and made honorable." When Justice saw Christ hanging on the tree " in the likeness of sinful flesh," He was satisfied ; but if He had not seen a man on the Cross, He would would have said, " How is this ? This is not the representative of sinners. He bears no resemblance to them ; their proxy must be a man." This was taught by the brazen serpent. The serpent, you know, has been the emblem of sinners ever since man became a sinner. It is the family crest of that great serpent, the Devil, and its brazen *effigy*, therefore, shows that sinners must be saved by one in the *likeness* of a sinner.

> " Jesus for us a body took,
> Our guilt assumed, our bondage broke,
> Discharging all our dreadful debt —
> Then let us ne'er this love forget."

Allow this to have been his first reason for becoming man, and I willingly admit that *to set us an example*, was another. God never made but two pattern men, and the first was soon spoiled as an example. The other held fast his integrity to the end. He was like those pictures, which retain their tone from age to age, and whose beauties are only mellowed by time. Some men set a good example at one period of life, but not at another. In certain circumstances they act well, but not in all. The lustre of one or two graces in their character is dimmed by numerous defects. But there was no inequality in the conduct of Jesus Christ, it was equally and perfectly good under all circumstances. In his character there was a union of every excellence, and each excellence was carried to its highest pitch, and, above all, there was not a flaw, nor a blemish, nor a fault, to mar, weaken, or abate the effect of his virtues. They shone with the brilliancy of the star-studded heavens, in a cloud less night, and with the distinctness of the rainbow in the painted sky. Do you say that such a copy is too perfect to follow ? Amend that, if you please, by saying that it is too perfect to equal. It may, and must be followed, even if we follow it afar off. A man may make a bad copy of a good picture. If he cannot match the original he may at least do something like it. Very few copies are equally, and in all respects like the original. There is a strong resemblance in one feature, perhaps, and not in another. So Christians differ in their likeness to Christ. A very few are so like him, that they are "living epistles of himself, known and read of all men." Others are noted, as John, for being like him in courage; or as Paul, for being like him in zeal. If ye cannot copy him to the life, we must do our best, for he became man, to leave us an "example that we should follow in his steps."

> "O, Saviour, till my life shall end,
>   Be thou my Counsellor and Friend ;
>   Teach me thy precepts all divine,
>   And be thy great example mine."

But once more, Christ became man that he might have for us a *fellow-feeling*. Some have thoughtlessly said that if Christ felt as a man, He must have had very sinful feelings. I admit that if he had assumed our fallen nature, this would have been the case, but, although Christ was our fellow man, he was not our fellow sinner. He assumed the nature of man as it was given by God, not as it was marred by sin, and the feelings which He had in common with us were like those of Adam in Paradise. Take an instance in which He displayed such feelings. Do you see that man with a withered hand? It is the Sabbath day, and the enemies of Christ are watching to see how He acts. "Stand forth," says Christ, to the afflicted one. Then turning to his spies, he says— "Look at that poor creature; shall I break the Sabbath if I make him whole?" But "they held their peace." Now observe Christ's face and see what I mean by fellow feeling. Is there no displeasure in his eye? Is there no sorrow in his visage? Yes; and Adam might have felt as He did, under like circumstances. "He looked round about on them with anger, being grieved for the hardness of their hearts." This proves that to feel for sinners it is not necessary to be a sinner ; and what I understand by fellow feeling, is not only feeling as another feels, but feeling for one's fellow ; and the purer a man is, the more he has of this feeling. Who are they that go into cellars, and dungeons, and mad-houses, to relieve suffering ? Who are they that traverse the earth to console the miserable, to nurse the sick, and to bind up the wounds of the fallen? The Howards and the Frys and the Dixes, and the Florence Nightengales of the world, are the purest beings on the earth ; and on the same principle, Jesus Christ, because the purest of beings, was the most sympathizing. He became man that He might know, by actual experience, what as God he never could know—the nature of the evils we have to suffer. It is the greatest comfort on earth to know that Christ was a man, for, " We have not an High Priest that cannot be touched with the feeling of our infirmities," but one " who was in all points tempted like as we are, yet without sin."

II. Thus we have discussed the nature of Christ, as here presented to us. Let us pass on now to the *offices* which He is said to discharge. "*A man shall be as an hiding place from the wind, and a covert from the tempest.*" I understand by this, that Christ shelters us from ills, of which the wind and the tempest are emblems. The figure is taken from the caves in which persons hid themselves when pursued by enemies, as David did, for example, when pursued by Saul. It is said that even now, in the East, one who protects another is called " his hiding place." Christ may be called ours, for many reasons.

First, *He hides us from error.* I have heard persons say, "there are so many opinions about religion in the world that we cannot discern between right and wrong." Now go and tell Christ that—say unto him, "Lord, there are so many guide posts to heaven, that we cannot tell which is right." Men interpret Thy words in so many senses that we

cannot ascertain what is truth." What would Christ say to that? In
nine cases out of ten, He would say, "Thou art a blind man, let me
anoint thine eyes. What see'st thou? "Myself, my sins, my helplessness." "Anything else?" "Yea, Lord, I see Thee wounded and bleeding on a cross—I see hell opening to swallow me up; 'Lord save, or I
perish!'" Now can a man in that state of mind, be imposed upon to
believe a lie? Will you palm off upon him for good money the spurious
coin of any of the heresies in circulation? Can you make him believe
that there is no hell, when he feels himself to be standing on its very
brink? or, that Christ is not God, when convinced that nothing but an
Almighty arm can snatch him from perdition? I trow not. Show him
a piece of bad money. "Whose image and superscription is this?" he
would say. "Christ's." "Not so," he would answer, "I know Christ's
image; I saw him on the Cross, his head was crowned with thorns and
covered with blood; his face was marred by grief, and wet with tears;
this is not the head of Christ, it is Satan's head, away with it. Look at
the superscription—not I. H. S.—"Jehovah Hominum Salvator," but, S.
M. R.—"Sathanus Mendacium Rex." You cannot mislead such a man
as to the way to heaven. He has a compass, and chart, and sailing directions, from the King of heaven. Thus Jesus Christ hides us from
error, *by bringing us into a knowledge of the truth.* We can no more
tell the difference between truth and error in religion before Christ opens
our eyes, than a blind man can tell the difference between white and
black. "The natural man receiveth not the things of the Spirit for they
are foolishness unto him, neither can he know them, for they are spiritually discerned."

Again, Christ hides us from error *by giving us a humble, child-like
faith.* We stand much in need of a hiding place from the wind of false
doctrine. Multitudes are "carried about with every wind of doctrine,
ever learning, and never coming to the knowledge of the truth." How
is that? Because they are too proud to take Christ as their teacher, and

cleave lovingly and reverently to his words. I have seen a child contend for the truth of his father's words, until the tears ran down his cheeks. He not only believed them himself, but he was shocked at their being questioned by others. But there be many who think it beneath them to take it for granted that what Christ says is true. They are too " wise in their own conceit " for that. They have travelled all over Europe ; they have visited Egypt ; they have scaled the Pyramids ; They have explored the Catacombs ; they have been everywhere, but to the Cross. Ask them about Christ, and they will tell you that He was a good man, but that you must not believe all He says. No man is safe from error, who, when Christ has settled a point, presumes to form an opinion about it himself. I claim for Christ, what the Romanist falsely claims for his Church—infallibility. Ask a Romanist what he believes, and he will tell tell you, " I believe what the Church believes," and if you ask him what the Church believes, he will tell you, " The Church believes what I believe." This is what makes it so hard to argue with a Romanist. He runs up a tree for safety. He says the Church, the Church, to every thing. I praise not his blind, ignorant and misplaced confidence, but I say, that if you trusted Christ as fully as the Romanist trusts his Church, he would be unto you " as an hiding place " from error, a safeguard from " the sleight of men, and the cunning craftiness whereby they lie in wait to deceive." If you cling to Christ as limpets to the rock, you will not be devoured by monsters of the deep. He is a "hiding place." from error, when we simply trust what He says.

And, once more, he hides us from error *by providing us with an infallible test of truth.* There are some here, perhaps, to whom all opinions in religion are equally right. They would as soon sail under one flag, as another. How is that? Why, the fact is, that they are ignorant of the standard by which to judge of what is truth. You have never set down to ascertain what doctrines they are which Christ teaches, and thus you are unable to distinguish between right and wrong.

Pray let me ask you how you distinguish between a genuine note and a forgery? Do you not go to a Counterfeit Detector? In like manner consult your Bible, and you will detect the soundness or fallacy of religious doctrine. "If they speak not according to this word, it is because there is no truth in them." This is one sense, then, in which Christ is a "hiding place from the wind." He shields us from error, by changing our hearts, by opening our eyes, and by subduing our pride.

> " 'Tis the humble God protects,
> 'Tis the meek, his light directs,
> 'Tis the mourner, sings his song,
> 'Tis the weak, He renders strong,
> 'Tis the simple who are taught
> Wisdom passing human thought."

III. Christ hides us from *trouble.* "Many are the troubles," we are told, "of the righteous, but the Lord delivereth him out of them all." It is not so with the wicked, for, "the sorrow of the world worketh death." But none of Christ's vessels are lost. He is in that sense their "hiding place." They "are kept by the power of God unto salvation." He brings them home "through much tribulation." He brings them home, as Captain Kane brought home his boat "Faith," battered and beaten, I admit, but safe and sound nevertheless. Her return was very dubious; it hung upon the life, skill and intrepidity of a mere man, and upon a thousand hair-breadth escapes from danger. But whether the Christian will surmount his troubles, is not problematical at all. It does not tremble in the balance of contingencies, but it is secured by the faithfulness and irresistible power of God himself. When He says "Be still," the bellowing winds cease to roar, and the raging waves subside into a calm. There be many Christians who never get the comfort of that truth. Although Christ has delivered them out of a thousand troubles, they are as much scared by their last trial, as by the first that they ever met with. "Why are ye so fearful, O, ye of little faith."

> "Did ever trouble yet befall,
> And He refuse to hear thy call?

And has He not his promise passed
That thou shalt overcome at last?

2. Christ hides his people by *sustaining them when they are in trouble.* He has a thousand ways of doing so. One is *by giving them a refreshing sense of his presence.* Thereby their nerves are strengthened to bear trouble. He does not make them insensible to it. He refused a stupefying draft when He was himself in agony, and He gives them none. If He deadened their nerves so that they could not feel pain, how could his grace be glorified by their patience in suffering? It is not, I say, by stupefying them, that Christ sustains his people in affliction. He does so by making them feel that He is close by. He whispers in their ear, "It is I, be not afraid," and they will go through fire and water when they hear that. There is Peter walking on the waves with as much boldness as on the dry land, when Christ has hold of him. Listen to David: "When I pass through the valley of the shadow of death, I will fear no evil, for thou art with me, thy rod and thy staff, they comfort me." What is the secret of this courage? How is it that when they see him, Christ's people will go into the den of lions, or the fiery furnace, or march even to the stake or to the rack without flinching? Because to their faith his presence is a proof of safety—a pledge that however grievous their troubles, they will come out of them eventually unharmed. Would not the assurance of recovery enable you to bear the surgeon's knife? So in his afflictions the Christian is upheld by the assurance that they will all work together for his good. What amazing instances I could mention of the magical effect of Christ's presence upon his people in time of trouble! Look at Stephen on his knees, with his hands and eyes raised to heaven in joy and rapture. How is that? Are they not hurling stones at him? Yes, and they will hurl one presently that will give him his death-blow; but listen: "Behold," he says, "I see the heavens opened, and the Son of Man standing on the right hand of God." That is the secret. Again, I hear sweet strains

of music; they come from the common jail at Philippi. How is it that men in such circumstances can be singing Psalms? Are they deranged? They may be put to death on the morrow. It is Christ's presence that gives them "songs in the night." It is that sweet sense of security which caused the martyrs to carry fagots as though they were palm branches to the flames, and calmly sit down in their chariots of fire.

But let me take you to a scene that I have often witnessed. Step up those stairs, enter yon chamber;—that couch has been pressed for fourteen years, day and night, by a Christian maiden. I knew her well. She suffered tortures. How is it, then, that she has that sweet smile—that placid look—that calm, holy countenance? What gives her strength to employ every interval from pain in prayer with the prayerless, in teaching the ignorant, and in exhorting sinners? There she is; ask her how it happens that she can bear with the serenity of an angel her awful sufferings? "Christ in me the hope of glory," she says; "He is my hiding place from the wind, my covert from the tempest."

> "Jesus can make a dying bed
> 　Feel soft as downy pillows are;
> While on his breast I lean my head,
> 　And breathe my life out sweetly there."

My dear brethren, allow me to say that the faith which enables us to realize the presence of Christ on a death-bed is the very same faith which enables us to realize his presence anywhere. If you are in the habit of trusting in him, and of walking with him, and of living on him, before your last conflict, you will find it easy when it comes to do so again. If you have proved him faithful in the least trial, you will be bold to rely on him in the greatest of all trials. But if your faith has been kept like a sword in its scabbard until the last enemy attacks you, mayhap it will not come out of its sheath; or if it do, be so rusty and dull as not to cut. To die is to the eye of sense to leap into an unfathomable abyss—to embark on a shoreless sea—to land upon an unknown country. "Oh, sir," said a dying person to John Newton, " it is a serious thing to die ; no words can express what is needful to support the soul in the solemnity of a dying hour." Yes, it is the greatest trial that faith has to meet with ; and I beseech you to prepare for it by keeping your faith in sharp exercise. Oh, with what resolution will you throw yourselves into the arms of Christ when you come to die, if you have been in the habit of doing so before you were confronted by the King of Terrors !

IV. I have reserved the most important sense in which Christ is a hiding place to the last. He is *a hiding place from " the wrath to come."*

Do you see yon city on the plain ? Its gates are always open ; all lines of road leading to it are as straight and as smooth as art can make them ; there is nothing to trip up or impede the most urgent traveler. See, now, who is it comes panting at the top of his speed along the road ? Behold how he fastens his eyes on the city of refuge, and strains every muscle and nerve to reach its walls. Ah, he is pursued. A man, sword in hand, is close upon his track, nearly up to him. Run, man, run ! One effort more ! God be praised, he has escaped—he is within the walls ! The avenger of blood is at his heels but dare not touch a hair of his head—he is safe ! Now what does that mean ? Art thou out of Christ ? It means that thou art in danger of death—that thy life is forfeited to divine justice—that he is in full pursuit. It means that the way of salvation is plain, and it urges thee to escape for thy life to the only Saviour. Again, when the world was some two thousand years old, you might have seen four men, a father and his three sons, hewing timber. The woods resounded with their sturdy blows. " What are these people cutting down so many trees for ?" said the neighbors. " The Noah family are a queer set—let us go and see what they are about." They found Noah building an ark three hundred cubits long. " Mad man," they exclaimed, " what is this thou art doing ?" " Mad man !" he replied, " it

is not I, men and brethren, that am mad. It is madness to commit sin,
to corrupt yourselves, and to fill the whole earth with violence. It is
madness to provoke the Lord God to anger, and to bring down upon your
heads the fury of his wrath. What I am doing is by his appointment.
'Yet a little,' He hath said, 'and I will bring a flood of waters upon the
earth to destroy all flesh. Make thee an ark for the saving of thy house.'
Very shortly the sky will darken, and the storm burst, and no other
place under heaven be given among men whereby they may be saved
but this very ark. Flee from the wrath to come. Come to the ark for
safety, and it shall be unto you as an hiding place from the wind, and a '
covert from the tempest." What did this signify? The same as before.
It signified that God has provided a refuge for sinners against the wrath
to come, as he did against that which is past. It signifies that as the ark
was the only hiding place when the fountains of the great deep were
broken up, and the windows of heaven opened, so Christ will be the only
refuge when the chariots of fire shall rush from heaven, and the trumpets
of God call to Judgment. Thus, brethren, Jesus is a hiding place from
the tempest of God's wrath against sin. Naturalists say that in Australia there is an animal whose young, on the approach of danger, always
run into its parent's mouth. Without you destroy the mother you cannot destroy the offspring. So is the life of his people hid with Christ.
Because He lives they shall live also. They take refuge in him as the
fowls fly to their homes from the coming storm.

> " To its covert glides the silent bird,
> While the hurricane's distant voice is heard."

Learn two or three things from this subject. First, *That no sinner
will flee to Christ until he is sensible of his guilt and danger.* Christ
is a hiding place, and no man hides himself who feels safe. He must
have his fears aroused first. I remember no instance to the contrary in
the whole Bible. It was so with the publican, Mary Magdalen, the jail-

or, and the thief on the cross. As it was with the hero of Bunyan's allegory, so it is with every Christian. He does not set out on his pilgrimage until he feels it unsafe to dwell in the city of destruction. As soon as the burden of his sin becomes intolerable, he seeks to be relieved —not before. There are some here, perhaps, who were taught to pray as soon as they could lisp; they have heard the Gospel preached all their days, and yet not being convinced of sin, have never fled to Christ for refuge. Nor will they ever ask, " What must I do to be saved?" until they feel their need of salvation. Where are such feelings to come from? I am totally unable to excite them. A tongue of fire now kindling a holy fear in each heart that has hitherto been as hard as stone, and as cold as ice, would be a blessing; but tongues of fire come from God. I might drag back the somnambulist from the overhanging cliff—I might snatch the dreamer from a house in flames—I might arouse the passengers in a sinking ship; but I cannot make you flee from the wrath to come. God alone can do that. The preacher's words, like the cable wherewith they tried lately to underlay the ocean, will conduct well; but the lightning, my friends! Of what use is the cable without the lightning which comes down from heaven? One spark of that would set my words on fire, and kindle in every heart, though submerged in sin, a corresponding flame. Oh, for the outpouring among us of spiritual influences!

> "Come, Holy Ghost! Creator, come!
>   Inspire these souls of thine;
> Till every heart which thou hast made,
>   Be filled with grace divine."

Learn again, from this subject, *the importance of cherishing serious impressions.* In a dead calm the sailor takes advantage of a *breath* of wind. He says that what is now only a catspaw, may prove by-and-by to be a lively breeze. So serious impressions, because slight, should never be slighted. Who can tell but that they may lead you to Christ. Saving ones indeed are the work of the Holy Ghost, but still, as our

Lord says, **the** operations of the Holy Ghost are like the wind. They do not commonly break on you as a hurricane, but freshen from a mere zephyr, which just suffices to ripple the water, to a brisk gale that carries you into port. Never make light of serious impressions. As drowning men catch at straws, so perishing sinners should snatch at every hope of safety. Although but skin deep, they may be improved by God's blessing; but if you say as Felix did to them, "Go thy way for this time," they may never return. See that man yonder, how anxious he looks—how tearfully he listens to what I say; there is emotion in his face, and every indication of serious feelings. What does he do with them? Does he carry them to the closet and make them the subject of earnest prayer? No. Does he ask God to burn them in before they melt away like scratches on wax exposed to fire? No. He goes into the world—he laughs and talks them away—and of course they are temporary and short-lived. My dear friends, the warmest and most affectionate wish of my heart is that you may all take refuge in Jesus Christ; but you are greatly engrossed with business, and the world soon dissipates the warm feelings and good resolves awakened in the sanctuary. Take them, then, I beseech you, when fresh and newly formed, and ask God to give them depth and permanence. Watch over them lest they should be choked by the cares, pleasures, and plans of life. Tend them with the assiduity that the nurseryman gives the exotic plant, and then they may strike root downwards, and bear fruit upward, to the glory of God. Even your afflictions, if sanctified, may prove blessings. A heart broken by sorrow, may be made a broken and contrite heart; and the tears shed at a grave may be converted by prayer into precious pearls.

> " Afflictions from above,
>   Are angels sent on embassies of love.
>   A fiery legion at our *birth*,
>   Of chastening woes were *given :*

> To pluck the flowers of hope from *earth*,
> And plant them high
> O'er yonder sky,
> Transferred to stars and fixed to heaven."

Once more, this subject teaches that *Christ is God*. How could a mere man shield us from the tempest of divine wrath? What mortal could rescue sinners from a storm like that? It is preposterous to suppose that a mere man could receive the lightnings of the Almighty into his bosom, and remain unscathed himself, much less shield his fellows from destruction. But Christ passed through and came out of the storm unhurt, and so has proved himself to be truly God, as well as truly man, and to be as able as he is willing to save unto the uttermost all that come unto him.

And now, sirs, how many are there here who have fled to this refuge? In old times, if a criminal ran into a Church and clung to the altar, no one might do him any harm; he was said to have taken sanctuary, and so long as he remained there, he could not without sacrilege be put to death. Many, however, like Thomas à Becket found that kind of sanctuary insecure. But the refuge which I tell you of, my unconverted hearers, is absolutely inviolable. A troubled conscience cannot enter it, because sprinkled with the peace-speaking blood of Jesus; Afflictions and trials cannot destroy it, because full of comfort; turbulent passions are excluded from it; the swellings of Jordan cannot overflow it; and the tornado of the day of judgment will vainly rage and roar against it. You, who are out of Christ, remember that you are exposed to all of these evils. If you die in your sins,—and except you believe in Jesus, you will die in your sins,—you will stand reeking with guilt before God. There will not be a tongue to plead for you; there will not be an arm to protect you; the Judge will frown on you; fiends will exult over you, and you will call in vain upon the rocks and mountains to give you shelter. I warn you, then, before it is too late, to flee to Jesus, as the only "hiding place from the tempest, and covert from the storm." There He is bleeding, groaning and dying for your salvation. Look at him; believe on him ere the day closes, or the sun sets. May the Holy Ghost open your eyes to see the danger you are in, whilst exposed as Christless souls, to the wrath to come!

Many of you have already fled to Christ for refuge, my dear hearers. You can say we are the children of God, by faith in Christ Jesus. You can say I was born again, under such and such circumstances, and I remember the storm which drove me to the hiding place. It was at the bedside of a dying friend; it was at the grave of a beloved relative; it was under that preacher, or when I was laboring under such an afflic-tion. Well, then, be grateful for the escape you have met with. Praise God in your lives; by your works, and with your lips, and when your work is done here, you will praise him forever and ever with the Angels in heaven. AMEN.

THE SHOCK OF CORN.

"Thou shalt come to thy grave in a full age, like as a shock of corn cometh in in his season."—JOB v : 26.

THIS is a description of a good man's end. Sometimes, and in some respects, for the glory of God, it may be ordered otherwise, but it is generally true, and in one respect invariably so; the good man never fails to finish happily the journey of life. If I may use the expression, he arrives at the terminus of the celestial railway, not at the abyss which concludes the zig-zag road wherein the wicked travel. Or, to change the figure, however stormy may have been his voyage, he runs into port at last; he does not founder at sea, but gains the haven of peace and blessedness. But when I speak of a good man, I do not mean a good father, a good friend, or a good citizen. I use the word good in the sense which it bears in God's vocabulary, not in ours. I allude to imputed and imparted goodness, to that which is wrought for us, and to that which is wrought in us. The merits of Christ imputed to the sinner makes him good. A good man is, in Scripture language, one who is justified by faith, and sanctified by the Holy Ghost. Let each ask himself then, if, in this sense, he be entitled to the appellation, for if so, he may appropriate all the comfort of this assurance, "Thou shalt come to thy grave in a full age, like as a shock of corn cometh in, in his season." There are three clauses in the text, each of which deserves our attention.

I. First, "Thou shalt come to thy grave," and this is an opposition, I

take it, to an *untimely death*. Of some who are buried, it cannot be
said that they come to *their* grave because they shorten their lives by
sin. They are buried, perhaps, somewhere fifty years this side the grave
that rightfully belonged to them, and where they ought to have come in
the course of nature. This is what the Scripture means by saying that
"the wicked shall not live out half their days." Sin in the shape of
luxury, intemperance, ambition, lust, pride or passion cuts their lives
short. They would live as long again, otherwise. Good men, indeed,
may die early. They are often called to sacrifice their lives in the discharge of duty, as the missionary at his post, the martyr at the stake,
the patriot in the field, but they come to their grave nevertheless, for an
early death is not necessarily an untimely one. Our times are in God's
hands, and die when we may, our death in his cause and service is never
premature. But the case is very different with the suicide, or the
inebriate, or him who falls a victim to his fierce temper or foul tongue.
They rush into God's presence without a call. There was an account
in the papers lately of a poor man who, because bereaved, and out of
work lay down, by the side of his dead child and poisoned himself. Now
do you suppose that the man who succumbs in that way to worldly sorrow, who for the want of the support of faith sinks under misfortunes,
and puts an end to himself, cometh to his grave by divine appointment?
Or the contentious, who are killed by stirring up strife, or the youths
who are slain in drunken brawls, suppose ye that they owe their death
to the decree of heaven? I admit that the Governor of the world allows
those who commit sin to reap the consequences, but if they come to an
untimely end it is their own fault, for they are not obliged to its commission. It is not the Judge who condemns a man to the gallows who is
chargeable with his death, it is the malefactor who brought himself
there. But it is said, in contrast with all this, of the good man, "Thou
shalt come to thy grave," to that whereunto he was ordained, for his
years are not shortened by excess or violence, he has no vices to destroy

his health, he controls his passions, curbs his temper and bridles his tongue. Whatever may be his troubles the good man says with Job, "All the days of my appointed time will I wait till my change come." Dr. Dwight's mother, when more than a hundred years old, burst into tears when she heard the bell toll for a funeral. "When will it toll for me?" she exclaimed, "I am afraid that I shall never die." This was as much as to say, "Lord now lettest thou thy servant depart in peace." I am weary of life, but I cannot throw it down without permission. I should welcome the tomb, but must not descend into it before the time.

"Thou shalt come to *thy* grave." Again, this implies that there is a *peculiarity about the Christian's grave.* As to the resting place of part of Christ's mystical body, it is a sacred spot. Though grown over with grass and nettles, it is holy ground, precious in the sight of God and angels, for it enshrines a gem that shall sparkle forever in the Saviour's crown. The grave levels, it is said, all distinctions, and truly there is no great difference to be seen among the mansions of the dead. The houses, although some may be a little finer than others, are all dark, cold and narrow. But unseen, there is a mighty difference, for from this grave, like his transfigured Lord, shall one come forth having his face shine as the sun and his raiment white as the light, whilst another shall arise from that to shame and contempt, this shall yield up an angel, and that a demon. From hence shall spring and soar to heaven, a glorified saint, whilst a lost sinner, crying out to the rocks for shelter, shall crawl from the other. Thus there is a peculiarity about the Christian's grave. Before Napoleon was entombed in Paris, I visited his grave. It was on a rock. Christ's sepulchre was in a rock, but it was not a sea-beaten rock, about which the waves broke and the winds howled. Napoleon's first grave was better suited to him as a warrior; he lived a stormy life and he had a stormy grave. The quiet tomb in the garden was better suited to Christ, as the Prince of Peace, and the rock of our salvation. I had sad and solemn feelings at Napoleon's grave,—for greatness in ruins is a melancholy sight,—but I did not feel that the ground whereon I stood was holy ground, as I should at that of Washington. It is always thus. The graves of the wicked are often regarded with contempt, but you behold those of the just with respect and reverence. You feel that their useful, holy and devoted lives confer sacredness upon their sepulchres, they are hallowed spots. Ah, brethren, many a proud mausoleum has been reared to wealth ; many a pompous epitaph has been inscribed to genius ; many a gorgeous monument has been raised to majesty, but a good man's grave, though only covered with turf and bound with osiers, has a dignity that no marble can confer, no sculptor adorn, no poetry ennoble. " Thou shalt come to thy grave."

But these words may be taken literally. Not to be buried was considered disgraceful, both by the Jews and Gentiles. On this account, the Romans threw the bodies of criminals into the Tiber, and pretended that the souls of the unburied dead wandered about seeking rest, but finding none, for a hundred years. The reproach which the Jews attached to the want of sepulture is plain from Scripture. Listen, for instance, to God's sentence on Jehoiakim. " He shall be buried with the burial of an ass, drawn and cast forth beyond the gates of Jerusalem ;" and to that of Jezebel, "the dogs shall eat Jezebel in the portion of Jezreel, and there shall be none to bury her." The grave, it is true, is common property, and our civilization allows a grave to every one. It is the house appointed for all living. Many a good man, moreover, has been consigned without shroud or coffin to the deep. Many a martyr has been burnt to ashes, which, like those of Wickliffe, have been scattered to the winds. But the rule is, that he who lives piously shall be buried honorably ; that devout men shall carry him, as they did Stephen, to his burial ; that friends and fellow citizens, with tears and regrets, and funeral rites, shall lower his body into its place of rest. Thus the text has a literal meaning.

But, once more, the Christian comes to his grave, in the sense of *being willing to die.* Matthew Henry says, that the child of God "may play upon the hole of this asp, and put his hand upon this cockatrice's den." True, for to the child of God, death has no sting. Whenever he comes to him, it is on a friendly errand. In ancient times when a leper was healed, his house was demolished; and to the Christian, death is only the demolisher of his house of clay. Death says to him, "this house is no longer fit for thee to inhabit—it is tainted—I am sent to take it down and remove thee to 'a house not made with hands, eternal in the heavens.'" Coming on such an errand. the believer is not afraid of death. A Christian, in his last moments, when his friends said to him "how hard it is to die," answered, "Oh, no, easy dying, blessed dying, glorious dying." This is what I call coming to the grave. Payson came to his grave, when he exclaimed with his dying breath, "The celestial city is full in view—its breezes fan me—its odors are wafted to me—its music strikes upon my ear, and its spirit breathes into my heart." I understand coming to the grave, as opposed to being dragged there. The sinner is like some criminals I have read of, who, refusing to walk, had to be carried to execution; but the Christian makes no resistance. Sinners cannot bear to hear death mentioned in their hearing. They have even intoxicated themselves at its approach. They have asked if death could not be bribed. I have read of one who exclaimed, "I won't die now; I am determined I won't die, I will live." Thus they strive and struggle with death, as a man arrested might do with an officer of justice. But look at the dying Christian—hear him bid farewell to his weeping family, telling them he can go no further; that his pilgrimage is ended; exhorting them to meet him in a brighter world, and then exclaiming, with eyes upraised to heaven,

> " To Jesus the crown of my hope,
> My soul is in haste to be gone;
> O! bear me ye cherubim up,
> And waft me away to his throne."

Even the untutored Indian, in the prospect of death, experiences this peace when he is converted to God. An aged Christian chief was asked by a friend when they should meet again. "I am old," he replied; "I shall soon lie down," making signs of lowering a body in the grave, "but," pointing up to heaven, he exclaimed, "we shall meet with Jesus." Thus the Christian comes to his grave in the sense of not being afraid to die. He regards death as only the signal for him to depart, and "be with Jesus, which is far better."

II. Now the next clause, "Thou shalt come to thy grave in a full age." This reminds us that "the days of our age are three score years and ten;" but a full age does not necessarily mean a long life. I understand the text to say that the Christian *shall not die too soon.* It is sometimes asked, Why did such an one die in the prime of life?—as if a long series of years were necessary to prepare us for death. Seneca, although a heathen, knew better than that, for he tells us that "life is to be measured by action, not by time." "A man may die old," he says, "at thirty, and young at four score." But a Christian, die when he may, is full of age, because God does not will that he should live longer. One of you has lost a child, and you think that it was taken before the time, but how can that be if it was taken away by divine appointment? Has not he lived long enough who lives as long as God pleases? Suppose that a certain man planted trees on an estate remote from that where he resided, with the view of removing them at a proper season to his own orchard. He knew infallibly when they ought to be removed, and he had the power of transplanting them at any period. Suppose such a case; would you find fault with him because the finest trees were often allowed to stand for years, whilst he removed some of them when mere seedlings? Would you object that the first were too old and the last too young for removal? No; you would say, rather, that whether old or young, they were removed at the proper time, at a full age. You would say that such was the proprietor's skill there could be no mistake. You might be unable to tell his reasons, or to explain the principles on which he acted. You might account for their removal by their great promise, or by their hindering the growth of the neighboring trees, or because it was likely they would perish otherwise; but if you had confidence in the man, you would not doubt that he removed the trees at the proper time, and that it would have been unfit for them to continue in the plantation a moment longer. Just so it is with the removal of God's people from earth to heaven. It is not their age which God regards in removing them, but the ends and purposes which He has in view. And knowing his goodness and wisdom, can we doubt for a moment that those ends justify their removal? No; God's time is the best time, be it close at hand or far off; and when it happens, no matter how old we are, we are full of age. Very often this age is attained by a mere child. I see a poor boy, eight or nine years old, always in church, and no one can tell me who he is. He disappears after service like a flash, but he is never absent from the house of God. At length I am called to visit a sick child. The messenger tells me of his "wonderful boy," so much beyond his years, says the old man, that "his conversation is out of my reach. He talks a great deal about things that I do not understand." On going to the house, I find in the little patient my mysterious hearer, and as I approach the straw on which he lays, he raises himself up, and stretching forth his arms, he exclaims, "His own right hand hath gotten himself the victory," and immediately expires. That once actually happened to a clergyman, and I call that boy of full age. On the other hand, many come not to a full age until they have passed through a long life of labor and usefulness. Wesley was not of full age until he had preached the Gospel sixty-five years; nor Luther, until for thirty years he had fought with Popery. Why a full age should be reached at the third hour by some, and not until the eleventh hour by others, I am unable to explain; but happen when it may, the hour of dissolution, if arranged by God, cannot be mistimed. "Shall not the Judge of all the earth do right?" Thus, whether he die early or late, the Christian never dies too soon. "Thou shalt come to thy grave in a full age."

Let me point out a few particulars in respect of which the Christian never dies too soon. And, first, he never dies too soon *for his own good.* In how many instances are "the righteous taken away from the evil to come!" Was it too soon for Jacob to die? Would you have had him live to see his descendants slaves, groaning under their burdens, scourged with whips, driven by taskmasters, and their little ones slain or cast into the Nile? Oh! there is love in the hand which by closing the Christian's eyes in death, hides from him the calamities that are drawing near. What distress and misery, are in this way, often spared to him! Look at that dying mother. Ask her if she be willing to die? "All that binds me to life," she replies, "are my children. It is only for their sakes that I wish to live." And then she bursts into tears and prays God to prolong her days, to see them happy. And yet it turns out afterwards, perhaps, that had her days been prolonged, she would have seen them wretched, broken in health, reduced in circumstances, or even lost in character. That she would have been called to watch for years at their bedside, or consign them, bereft of reason, to the care of strangers. It proves that had her life been lengthened, a messenger would have come to her, saying, "Thy sons and daughters are dead, they were crushed on the road, or drowned in the river, or perished at sea." Had she the foreknowledge of what was to happen, in place of desiring to live longer, she would say, "I have lived long enough, spare me the sight of these calamities.,' But there is another benefit of death to the Christian. It ends his warfare with sin and Satan. He never dies too soon for his own good, who is released by death from the necessity of perpetual vigilance; who is obliged, as long as he lives, to guard against sins of temper, tongue and affections! to keep the door of his lips, the issues of his heart, and the outlet of his thoughts with all diligence ; who must be always on the watch against foes without as well as enemies within, against the temptations of the world, the snares of Satan, and the cunning craftiness of wicked men. So long as he lives, the Christian is like a shipmaster at sea. He is haunted by care and overlaid with anxiety. He cannot safely, for a moment, remit his vigilance. Argus-eyed, he must be now on the forecastle, now at the wheel, and now in the maintop. His crew, his cargo, his sails, his rigging, the clouds, the winds and the treacherous deep, to him are all sources of solicitude. Sometimes he is startled by the cry of "fire, in the hold !" or "breakers ahead !" To-day he is in danger of shipwreck ; to morrow of capture, and then of mutiny. Oh ! it is a happy day for a sailor when he casts anchor, furls his sails, and pulls ashore. And so it is, with the believer, when he gets to heaven. He is freed by death from the dangerous navigation of life's stormy sea. He need no longer trouble himself to mortify the flesh, to keep under the body. The body with all its corruptions and infirmities is dead and buried, and henceforth he has no need to watch over the manifestations of inbred sin. He is safe—his poor bark, after tossing about, and running the gauntlet through a thousand enemies, is sheltered at last in the port of Heaven. If angels joy when they see a sinner homeward bound,—when they see the prow of his ship turned toward heaven,—how much more must sinners rejoice when they get there ! They that do that never die too soon for their own good.

> "Oh, when we gain the land,
> How happy shall we be,
> How shall we bless the mighty hand
> That led us through the sea.

Again, the Christian never dies to soon *for God's glory*. All men are timed with a view to that, because God's glory is their chief end ; what He mainly designed in their creation. I asked a watch maker the other day by what standard his clocks were regulated; what he regarded as the true time? God's glory is the regulator of all events, the standard time of the universe. In a large city you hear the clocks striking the hour at different times, but all our times keep pace exactly with God's chronometer. Nothing happens a moment sooner than his glory requires; nothing lasts a moment longer than his glory indicates. You may think, perhaps, that the long suffering of God with the wicked, is an exception. He certainly treats them with much forbearance. But this seeming departure from the rule is owing to the intercession of Jesus Christ, who pleads for its temporary suspension. God's glory does not demand the destruction of sinners so long as a chance remains of their repentance, because thereby it would be secured. So long as his good ness may lead them to repentance, it is continued, and his patience glorifies his grace; but the rule goes into effect at last, should the reprieve be useless. They never die until God's glory makes it necessary. There be some who regard life only as the period during which they may enjoy themselves. They would not think five hundred years long enough to live, if, without growing helpless and infirm, they could live a thousand. But the truth is that the object of life is not enjoyment. "God hath made all things for himself," for his own glory. And, in place of pleasure, it may be for God's glory, that we should live in torture, glorify him in the fires, toss for years on a bed of languishing, die in childhood, or live to old age. Was it not for God's glory that Stephen was stoned, and the innocents slain, and the martyrs burnt, and the Prophets killed? None of them died too soon, because they all lived as long as God's glory required. How many events, otherwise mysterious, may be thus accounted for! The early removal, for instance, of such men as Kirke White, Henry Martyn, Summerfield or Dudley Tyng,—the sundering of pious parents from their helpless families,—the death of ministers in the prime of life. What other reason can we assign for these apparently calamitous events, than the one I have mentioned?

There are doubtless the best reasons why such suns should set before culminating; reasons which, if known, we should approve; but this includes them all—it was more for God's glory that such persons should die, than that they should live.

III. We come now to the comparison of a dying Christian to a shock of corn. "Thou shalt come to thy grave as a shock of corn cometh in in his season." I shall not dwell long here, but the points of the similitude are very striking. The Christian, like the shock of corn, has experienced many changes. He has been changed from a sinner, into a saint, a transformation greater even than that of a grain of corn cast into the earth. He has passed through the various stages of spiritual growth, as the corn of natural. As it was, "first the blade, then the ear, after that the full corn in the ear;" so hath he grown from a babe to "the measure of the fulness of the stature of Christ." His growth, moreover, like that of the grain, has been fostered by heavenly influences. Be not surprised at the afflictions of the righteous, for, as the rough usage which the corn meets with before it reaches maturity is of the greatest consequence to the future crop, so, in their sanctifying effect on his soul, the Christian's trials prepare him for heaven, and make him meet for the inheritance of the saints in light. His losses, bereavements, sickness and other trials, are to him, what the vicissitudes of the weather are to the future harvest. As the most rugged plants are those which have stood out all winter, so they are the most eminent Christians who have grown in the open field of adversity. Affliction ripens the graces of their Christian character. They are so eminent for their faith, holiness and virtues, as to show, long before they die, that they are advanced, and readier than others for the sickle. The dying Christian, in short, like the shock of corn, is ready to be harvested. You can see that by his humility. His spirit is bowed down, as the cornstalk is inclined, by the weight of the ripe ear to the earth.

Many have gone to the bedside of a dying Christian, thinking to hear

him speak of his labors and sacrifices in the cause of Christ, of what he
has done for the Church, for the poor and the afflicted. They have expected that he would refer to his integrity in business, to his fair dealing,
and good morals; talking of these as a conqueror might talk of his vic-
tories. But in place of that, they have been amazed to hear him speak
of himself as a poor sinner, an unprofitable servant, without any other
dependence than God's mercy. When a friend reminded George Herbert
of his charities, he replied, "They be good works if they be sprinkled
with the blood of Christ, but not otherwise." When they brought to
the learned and pious Bede, on his death-bed, the Scriptures which he
had translated, he exclaimed, "Glory be to the Father, Son, and Holy
Ghost," and expired. Thus the dying Christian, like a shock of corn,
is bowed down. He is humble, lowly, meek, and boasts of nothing but
Christ crucified. He is ready to be harvested—he is ripe for heaven.
This is seen by his readiness to depart. In this, too, he resembles the
shock of corn; for when fully ripe a mere touch will bring the yellow
grains to the ground. He pants to be relieved; he says with Simeon,
"Lord, now lettest thou thy servant depart in peace;" or with Stephen,
"Lord Jesus, receive my spirit." What wonderful illustrations of this
might be quoted. "I am ready, I am ready," cried a dying Christian.
"Come, Lord Jesus, open, open the gate to thy servant." "I rejoice,"
said another, "to feel these bones give way; as it tells me I shall shortly be with my God in Glory." And that after all, brethren, is the chief
point of analogy; the Christian's death is like the *coming in* of a shock
of corn. The Moravians, I believe, are the only Christians who conduct
the funerals of believers on this principle. It is white, the color of the
wedding garment, that predominates at their burials; and so it should
be, for "harvest home" is a joyful period among all nations. Brethren,
they are continually having harvest in heaven. Were our eyes opened,
we should always see the air filled with angels bearing sheaves in their
bosom from all parts of the world to God's granary. And oh, what re-

joicing is there in the mansions above, as precious souls, borne in the arms of angels, approach their precincts! If they rejoice in heaven at the conversion of sinners, how much more must they exult at their salvation!

To conclude, observe what a change must be wrought in the soul ere it can go to heaven. There are thousands of the Lord's people who are now living in sin and impenitence, and were they to die now they would perish. Before dying they must be born again; they must be convinced, converted, and sanctified. Until then they are immortal, for they must not die until, like a shock of corn, they are ripe for the garner. Let us learn from the subject to prepare for death. He must soon come with his sickle, and whether for the harvest of wrath or happiness, is suspended on our being prepared to die. Oh, "may we die the death of the righteous, and may our last end be like his." May we be found, when death comes, ripe for heaven, covered with the blossoms of faith, and the fruits of righteousness!

> " Corn fully ripe is reaped and gathered in ;
> So must ourselves when ripe in grace or sin."

ABRAHAM'S TRIAL.

"And it came to pass after these things that God did tempt Abraham.' —GEN-
ESIS xxii.: 1.

ABRAHAM was born more than two thousand years before Christ. He
did not begin to live spiritually, however, until he was seventy-five years
old, and no doubt he regarded all that time as a blank in his existence,
for no man begins to live to any purpose until he lives to God. I have
read that a certain person converted at eighty, being asked his age, replied, "Little more than two years old, reckoning from the time when
I was born again." Many things that happened to Abraham had a spiritual meaning. Thus, his departure by God's command, from his country and kindred and father's house, denoted the call made on sinners in
the Gospel to forsake the world and set out at once as pilgrims to heaven ;
and so it was implied, by his dwelling in a strange land, that Christians, although they live in the world, do not belong to it. Even to his
children there was attached a mystic meaning ; one standing for the covenant of works, wherein a man goes out like Ishmael, to earn a living by
his own exertions; the other for the covenant of grace, in which he remains at home like Isaac, and subsists on the bounty of his father's
house. As for Abraham himself, he is proposed as a pattern to all believers, and the most illustrious example of faith and piety. Of these the
narrative before us is a striking instance, and as such it is commended to
us in the word of God. We shall follow its course, and comment as we
proceed, on its leading features.

I. "And it came to pass after these things that God did tempt Abraham."

The things referred to comprehend the events of his life from his leaving Haran to his settlement in Beersheba—such events as his exile, wars, hardships, and bereavements, making altogether a most painful history. But happily human life, like the desert, is interspersed with oases, and Abraham at length, having ceased from wandering, seemed to have the prospect of a happier future. But things often turn out very differently from what we expect. The merchant may die on his way home to enjoy his fortune; the ship may be blown out to sea when in sight of port; the cup may be dashed to the ground when raised to the lips. It was "after these things;" if I may so express myself, after he had made his fortune, retired from business, had nothing more, apparently, to encounter, and had weathered all the storms of life; it was "after these things that God did tempt Abraham." But is not that contrary to what St. James says of God, "Neither tempteth he any man?" Not at all; because St. James speaks of a different kind of temptation. Here the word "tempt" is used in the sense of trial; but St. James means by it to influence, move, or draw a man into sin. Never in that sense, he says, does God tempt any one. Satan does; he not only holds up the golden apple, the forbidden fruit, but he secretly invites us to pluck it off; he not only adapts his temptations to our tastes, but he provokes our tastes to yield to his temptations. He so plays his shining bait that we are taken as a fish in the net, as a fowl in the snare, or as a moth in the flame. Thus, like the Africans that Dr. Livingstone speaks of, Satan, after making a pitfall for his game, drives them into it; but God never does that. He only tries the strength of our faith for his glory, and our own good. I have read somewhere that the Sandwich Islanders believe that the strength and valor of the enemies they kill pass into themselves, and we are certainly gainers by every temptation which we overcome. Even failure may have the effect of putting us on our guard another time. The mariner may be wrecked to-day, but will it not cause him to be wary to-morrow? Trials sent to us for these ends, to prepare and purify our souls for heaven, are very different from those intended to increase our sins and bring down upon our heads a sorer punishment. The first are designed to make us happy, the last to engulph our souls in guilt and misery.

II. But how did God tempt Abraham? "Take now thy son, thine only son Isaac, whom thou lovest, and get thee unto the land of Moriah, and offer him there for a burnt-offering upon one of the mountains which I will tell thee of."

Observe what a sharp trial this was to his *faith*. "Abraham was a hundred years old when his son Isaac was born unto him." He was the child of many prayers. Oh, how his father had prayed for this boy! "Lord God," he had said, "behold, to me thou hast given no seed." "What wilt thou give me, seeing I go childless?" He was the child of many promises. On a starry night God had taken Abraham abroad, and, pointing him to the heavens, had told him that his seed should be as the stars for multitude. But last of all he was the child of the covenant. "My covenant," God had said, "will I establish with Isaac." "In Isaac shall thy seed be called;" and that seed, we are told, was Christ; so that in this promise Abraham saw the day of Christ, and "was glad." In this promise he saw the earth covered with Gospel blessings, and salvation for himself and all believers. What a paradox, then, was presented to his faith when God commanded him to slay his son! What an apparent repeal and repudiation of his engagements! Those who have felt puzzled to harmonize one doctrine of the Bible with another, such as God's sovereignty and man's freedom; those who have felt the struggle of faith with reason on meeting with seeming inconsistencies in the word of God, may fancy how the antagonism of the command and promise must have staggered Abraham. "Can I have heard aright?" he would say. "Can it be possible that the Author of a command and promise so much at variance with one another should be the same?" Thus it was a sharp trial to his faith. And so it was to his *feelings*.

You who have lost children can vouch for that. Oh, what sorrow the death of a child occasions! It is grief enough when Death plucks the full-blown rose, or cuts down the old tree, but who can help shedding tears when he nips the opening buds, or tramples under foot the spring flowers? You see the depth of that grief long afterwards. That bust on the table, the portrait on the wall, the inscription on the tomb, shows its poignancy. The most simple and affecting words I ever saw on a grave-stone were, "My only child;" and such was the epitaph that Abraham might have used had he lost Isaac. Oh, he might have chiseled words on the marble that would have waked the dead. "Sacred to the memory of my only son, born when his father was a hundred years old, and his mother ninety. With him all hopes of the salvation of sinners perished. He was the child of broken promises and unverified predictions. From him was to have sprung the seed that should bruise the serpent's head. In him was pledged to his parents a countless progeny; through him all the nations of the earth were to have been blessed; but he died without issue in the twenty-fifth year of his age." Ah, it was no common loss that seemed to threaten Abraham. It was the loss of his son—of his only son—but worst of all, of a son on whose life depended his own salvation, and that of all the people of God. And besides that he was his beloved son. Ah, God knoweth where to shoot his arrows. He touches Abraham in the tenderest part. It is those we love best that we are in danger of losing. If ye doubt that, go into the burial-place allotted to children; see how many blighted hopes, how many Isaacs, how many mothers' idols are there deposited! Abraham had good cause to love Isaac; the youth was dutiful and affectionate, his father's friend, and a shaft for his old age to lean upon; above all he was a child of God, and a bright example of early piety. These and a thousand other circumstances endeared Isaac to Abraham, and would in any shape have made his death distressing. Oh, the agonies he felt then on hearing not only that Isaac must die, but that his father's hand must slay him; that the author of his being must take it away, that he must lead Isaac like a sheep to the slaughter, bind him, put him to death, burn him to ashes, treat him just like a beast offered for sacrifice. That he must be the priest and Isaac the victim! Truly it was a sharp trial. When your children die you are allowed to smooth their pillow, and to do all you can to relieve their sufferings, but poor Abraham, in place of averting, must strike the blow—in place of healing must inflict the wound. But was it not harsh in God to prescribe such a task to Abraham? Never call it harsh in God to prescribe anything. He may have reasons for afflicting, which, if we only knew them, our heaviest trials would seem blessings. What better reasons can He have than his own glory and our good? "It is the chief end of man to glorify God," and Abraham glorified God by submission to his will and faith in his promises. God was glorified by his sufferings because he bore them obediently, patiently, trustingly. Besides, God's design in afflicting Abraham was to preach Christ crucified, when as yet faith had no cross to look at, no Bible to read, no Gospel to joy over. To denote that in the fullness of time, God would act Abraham's part, and Christ Isaac's in this transaction. In such a cause, and for such ends, Abraham might well rejoice that he was "counted worthy to suffer." Moreover, his sufferings were for his own benefit. They made him famous, they exalted him to the skies, they won for him the name of God's friend, the Father of the faithful, the founder of a nation, the progenitor of Christ. Thus in place of severity it was mercy in God to afflict Abraham, for as "there is no operation too severe that ends in health," so no trial can be called cruel that ends in glory.

III. But to proceed. "And Abraham rose up early in the morning, and saddled his ass, and took two of his young men with him, and Isaac his son, and prepared the wood for the burnt-offering, and rose up and went to the place of which God had told him." Notice his *promptitude;* he obeyed at once. Since he had no power to deviate from the course prescribed to him, it was safer for him to set out immediately, for a painful duty if put off to-day is less likely to be done to-morrow. Suppose Abraham had said, "I must think about it, I must consult my friends;" they would have dissuaded him, perhaps, from offering Isaac. "This thing," they might say, "will ruin your credit. What a scandal it will bring on religion, what grief to Sarah, what misery to yourself! How can you believe that God requires of you what He punished in Cain? If wrong for Cain to kill Abel, can it be right for Abraham to kill Isaac?" How fatal such reasoning might have proved had Abraham consulted with flesh and blood! Happily God's will was his rule of action, and that being ascertained he consulted no one. He arose at daybreak, and stealing from his tent for fear of Sarah, he awakened Isaac, and set out forthwith on his doleful errand. Learn from Abraham, my brethren, to make what sacrifices God requires without a pause. "Stop not at the threshold." Many a man is lost by this who might escape otherwise. God says to him, "My son, give me thine heart," but he takes time to think—he is assailed by doubts. Like the Arab who could not bring himself, though he was starving, to part with his steed, so the love of the world and of sin keeps him from Christ. He cannot make up his mind to part with Isaac, and so while he falters death decides, and snatches away from him the power of choice.

> " Procrastination is the thief of time.
> Year after year it steals, till all are fled; '
> And to the mercies of a moment leaves
> The vast concerns of an eternal scene."

But let us watch these travelers. They say little; the patriarch is sad and thoughtful. Each time he looks up he sees Isaac going like a sheep to the slaughter, and perhaps, as the unsuspecting lamb will "lick the hand just raised to shed his blood," so Isaac's face was lit up with a sunny smile when his father noticed him. Ah, how much easier it would have been for Abraham to kill Isaac at once, than have journeyed three days with him to the altar! All that time he had to think and brood over the task assigned to him. All that time he had to struggle with the remonstrances of nature and a father's feelings. Yes, but unless his trial had been thus exasperated, the power of his faith would have been less conspicuous. An anchor that will hold well enough for a while may give away at last. Abraham's faith was his anchor, and he rode by it for three days, though it blew a hurricane. That proved its strength, and that his trust in God was firm as a rock, and stronger than death.

IV. "Then on the third day Abraham lifted up his eyes and saw the place afar off."

There was not an object in view, brethren, but what was destined to become renowned and sacred. He saw the mountains that were to surround Jerusalem, the hills whereon it should be built, the heights of Olivet, the valley of Cedron. But it was not on these that Abraham's eye chiefly rested; he saw "the place that God had told him of," whereon a thousand years afterwards the temple was to shine in all its glory. He saw a cloud-capped mountain, the symbol of God's presence crowned its summit and revealed its selfness, The great altar of burnt-offering perhaps stood there afterwards, and no great way off was Calvary itself; this spot being chosen for Abraham's trial, to teach men that the sacrifice of beasts was only typical, that the true sin-offering mus be a man.

> " That blood on Jewish altars spilt,
> Could not atone for human guilt;
> That God's dear Son must bleed and die,
> To ransom souls from misery."

But look at Abraham! There he stands like a warrior reconnoitering the battle-field. Yonder is the signal cloud beckoning him onward.

Many a man, brave on the march, will take to flight when he sees the enemy, but he is not dismayed by the approaching crisis. "There is the place," thought Abraham; "I must climb those hills, I must carry Isaac into the jaws of the lion, but oh, my God, are not thy truth and promise pledged for his protection? Thus it is, brethren, that God's people can look danger in the face without flinching. They feel safe; strong in God and in the power of his might, they are brave as lions and quiet as lambs. Under the shadow of God's wing they regard their enemies as powerless. They look upon them as spent balls, or as spiked guns, or as chained beasts. When the Lamb of God stood in presence of the Roman Governor, Pilate was amazed at his fearlessness. "Knowest thou not that I have power to crucify thee and have power to release thee?" said Pilate. Jesus answered, "Thou couldest have no power at all against me except it were given thee from above." So it was with Daniel when they cast him into the lion's den. He did not move a muscle; "their mouths are shut," thought Daniel, "I am not afraid." So it was with David when he assailed Goliah. "I will give your flesh unto the fowls of the air, and to the beasts of the field," cried the giant. David answered, "No fear; I defy thee in the name of the Lord of Hosts." And in after times the power of faith to sustain and embolden God's people in time of peril has been often illustrated. See Luther, like a lamb among wolves, at the Diet of Worms. He was as firm and serene as in his cloister at Erfurth. "We who put our trust in the Lord of life and death," said Luther, are "Lords both of life and death." "I would have entered Worms," he said, "though there had been as many devils in the town as there were tiles upon its roofs." And here we see Abraham fortified by the same confidence resolved to ascend Moriah, and at God's command even to destroy his child. So calm and collected was Abraham that his servants could guess by no falter of tongue or emotion of manner that he was disturbed. "Abide ye here with the ass," he said, "and I and the lad will go yonder and worship and come again unto you." Wonderful!

Yes, he speaks, you see, with as much assurance of his return as though it had already happened. Had he been asked on what grounds he spake so confidently, he would have said, " I rely on God's promise ;" and had he been asked again how, in case of Isaac's death, that promise could be realized, he would have answered, " I cannot say ; I have no idea. I believe that rather than that his word should fail, even were Isaac dead, God would bring him to life again." Thus it was faith in the truth and power of God that sustained Abraham. There would not have been half the merit in his obeying God with his eyes open as there was in his following him blindfolded. And now

VI. " Abraham took the wood of the burnt-offering and laid it upon Isaac his son ; and he took the fire in his hand and a knife, and they went both of them together."

It occurs to me, that if lookers on, we should have seen Isaac at this point in a more thoughtful mood than formerly. Of a sudden, methinks, he becomes very grave, as if he had something on his mind. He says within himself, " This is a heavy load, why not let one of the servants carry it? There must be some special reasons for laying it upon my shoulders. How am I to understand this long, sudden, and unsuspected journey? Cannot God be as well worshipped at home as on Mount Moriah? Above all, where is the lamb? How is it that my father, so mindful usually of all which relates to holy things, has forgotten the victim? I must speak to him—Father!" How it must have startled Abraham to hear his son's voice; for up to this time Isaac had been " dumb, and opened not his mouth." No doubt his father suspected what was coming, and perhaps prayed, like Sampson, " Strengthen me, I pray thee, only this once, O God." He might well do so. We often wonder how Herod's soldiers could resist the artless looks of the babes of Bethlehem, but Abraham has a harder task, for he must turn a deaf ear to his own child. He must give no heed to his endearing words and

winning ways. Nay, though he cries, "My father!" words which bring
tears to his eyes, which appeal to his love and claim his protection, he
must keep his purpose. Oh, what a pattern is Abraham to those who
love husband or wife or children more than God; whose principles are
weaker than their affections, and who are easily severed from the path of
duty! Abraham would do and suffer anything rather than disobey God.
How happy are all who can act thus!

There was no want of tenderness in Abraham's character. Isaac had
no sooner said "My father!" than he answered, "Here am I, my son."
What a wealth of affection is treasured up in *little* words! They are
sometimes as full of love as is the Persian rose of fragrance. "My
father!" "My son!" Nothing can be plainer than that Abraham and
Isaac loved each other! But let us hearken to Isaac, 7, 8. "Behold
the fire and the wood, but where is the lamb for a burnt-offering?
And Abraham said, My son, God will provide himself a lamb for a
burnt-offering." Isaac had been well taught; he knew that a pure,
harmless lamb was the most acceptable sacrifice. He had heard of Abel
and Noah offering lambs, and often at Beersheba he had witnessed sacrifices. But how Isaac's question must have distressed Abraham! Concealment was impossible, and I have no doubt that now he told Isaac
the whole story from beginning to end. And methinks that after explaining to him all the circumstances, he said to him "Art thou willing that
I should obey God's command? Age and infirmity cannot contend with
youth and sturdiness. Art thou willing to be bound upon the altar and
put to death?" And then methinks Isaac threw himself on his father's
neck, and sobbingly said, "God's will be done. Not as I will, but as He
will, be it done unto me." And there they stood, father and son, weeping
in each other's arms—the father comforting Isaac "by the comfort
wherewith" he himself was "comforted of God," saying to him, "God
will provide." Thus darkly hinting his hope of rescue. "God will pro- '
vide." "Is anything too hard for the Lord?" "With God all things

are possible." All their trust was in God. There was no more hope for Isaac, unless God sent deliverance, than there was for the poor souls who leaped into the sea from the burning "Austria," and clung mid ocean to spar for safety. Oh, my friends, there will come a time when, without we have a hope in God, there will be hope in no other. This goodly world of ours will be in flames, and all around it will be a sea of fire! May we look for deliverance from our troubles and trials to the same source as Abraham!

> " O Holy Saviour, Friend unseen,
> Since on thine arm thou bid'st us lean,
> Help us throughout life's changing scene,
> By faith to cling to thee."

IX. "And," now, "they came to the place which God had told him of, and Abraham built an altar there and laid the wood in order, and bound Isaac, his son, and laid him on the altar upon the wood." Here I must pause, for who can describe Abraham's feelings? He had gone great lengths, his son pale and motionless, with his throat bared, awaits the blow, the knife, is unsheathed and nothing remains but to inflict the wound. The death of youths, in general, compared with what threatened Isaac, is a happy scene. They are surrounded by friends, and breathe their last in a mother's arms; but poor Isaac lays alone on a bed of sorrows. They fall asleep, they enter into rest as the ship, with nearly exhausted impulse, glides to anchorage; but Isaac expects a violent death, and expects it, moreover, from his father's hand. And how we pity Abraham! He had the comfort, however, of knowing that Isaac's faith was as firm as his own. Methinks that kneeling down by him, he said, "My son, do you still trust in God?" "I do," he replies. "What notwithstanding all this? Do you trust in God, although he takes you away in the flower of youth by a violent death?" "Though He slay me yet will I trust in him." Oh what a consolation for Abraham! But must not his child's virtues have embittered the thought of losing him, and made it harder to part?" Aye, I doubt not, that when Abraham "stretched out his hand to slay his son," it shook like an aspen leaf; but then mark what happened. In that last moment, in that great extremity, in that awful juncture, a voice from heaven stayed his arm, arrested the blow. "Abraham!" it cried, "Abraham! Lay not thine hand upon the lad, neither do thou anything unto him, for now I know that thou fearest God, seeing that thou hast not withheld thy son, thine only son, from me." Oh, sirs, I believe, that the angels could not contain themselves when they heard that. When they saw Abraham loose Isaac, and heard him say, "This my son was dead and is alive again," I think all the angels shouted with joy. Thus was faith rewarded, Isaac restored, the promises renewed, and with a light and thankful heart Abraham and his son returned homeward.

But all this, as I said before, has a Gospel counterpart, and there is scarcely an incident in Isaac's story, that has not its match in that of Jesus. Was He not, like Isaac, an only and beloved son? Was not his birth a miracle, announced to Mary, as Isaac's was to Sarah, by a messenger from heaven? Jesus, indeed, was three years on his way to the place which Isaac reached in three days, but days stand for years in prophetic language. Look at this symbolical picture, drawn two thousand years before Christ, of the way of salvation. God saves sinners, by putting his Son in the sinner's place. See you not Abraham laying the wood on Isaac's shoulders? He had no other reason, perhaps, for doing so, than that his son was stronger than himself, but God meant by it, that as Abraham laid the wood on Isaac, so He would transfer our sins to Christ, that He would place them to his charge, and look to him for their penalty. Again, God saves sinners freely, for the sake of Christ, "not for their own works or deservings." Men, in all ages, have attempted, in a thousand ways, to provide for their own salvation, but God will provide himself a lamb for a burnt offering," said Abraham, and the words mean, when rightly interpreted, "The sinner can make no atone-

ment; no adequate satisfaction can be made by the sinner, God will pro.
vide himself "a full, perfect and sufficient sacrifice." The blood of bulls
and of goats cannot take away sin. Ye must be "redeemed by the
precious blood of Christ, as of a lamb without blemish and without spot."
Nor is the inability of sinners to save themselves, less strongly marked
out by another incident. Abraham and Isaac, you remember, went
alone to the place of sacrifice. All the servants were left behind, because
in the Covenant of Grace, the Father and Son are the only parties. The
Covenant was not made between God and sinners, but between God and
Christ, for the simple reason that sinners were unable to keep the covenant. They could neither satisfy the demands of the law for hell, nor
render the obedience which it required for heaven. If any one imagine
that because he is not as other men are—that because he is moral and
virtuous, compared with others—he will go unpunished, let him not be
deceived. Look at Abraham with a knife in one hand and fire in the
other. Will God spare the sinner and punish the saint? Will He
punish Christ as the sinner's proxy and let the sinner himself, out of
Christ, go free? Nay sirs, it was the blazing fire of God's wrath and
the gleaming sword of his justice that the Patriarch carried. It implied
that God will "by no means clear the guilty," that standing in the sinner's
place Christ should die by his own Father's hand; that in the capacity
of a just Judge and offended law-giver, God himself would put him to
death. Then again, if you marvel at Abraham for withstanding Isaac,
what think you of God for refusing Christ? When Christ prayed to
his Father, there was no reply. He prayed three times, saying, "O my
Father if it be possible, let this cup pass from me," but God was silent.
Abraham not withholding his son is one thing; God freely giving his
Son to die for sinners is another. Only think of God not sparing his
holy, harmless and beloved Son for sinners! Only think of his turning
a deaf ear to his cries, for the sake of such poor guilty creatures as we
are!—But whither are all those people hurrying from the gates of

Jerusalem? Who is in their midst, his brow mangled with thorns and his back seamed with lashes, and what is it he bears on his weary shoulders? Ah, sirs, it is not Isaac, but Christ, that we are now looking at. He bore, like Isaac, the wood to the place of suffering. Our sins were the fuel which sinners clave, and that kindled by divine wrath, slew Jesus. How resigned and submissive is the lowly Saviour—no murmur escapes his lips, He receives all their ill treatment without a word. See you not now why Isaac was so tractable; he would have been no type of Jesus otherwise. Jesus said, "Lo, I come to do thy will, O God. I lay down my life. No man taketh it from me, but I lay it down of myself." Jesus "gave his back to the smiters, and his cheeks to them that plucked off the hair." See how they throw him on the ground, and fasten him with nails to the accursed tree! No friendly voice stay their hands, no God sent substitute saves his life. For thy son, O Abraham, there was found a ransom, but for the Lamb of God's providing, entangled in the impenetrable thickets of our sins, there was no deliverance. And yet, after three days, He rose again. Isaac after being for that time esteemed as good as dead, was rescued; and Jesus after being for that time truly dead, was quickened. Yea, and to crown all, He went home, like Isaac, to his Father's house, and no doubt, as He came, the attending angels bid the ancient gates to lift up their heads, that the King of Glory might come in, and the souls of the just, made perfect, shouted "Worthy is the Lamb that was slain, to receive power, and riches, and wisdom, and strength, and honor, and glory, and blessing."

Finally, the great lesson taught us by this narrative is, that the principle of true obedience is faith, and that the mark of true faith is obedience. "Now I know that thou fearest God," said the Lord to Abraham. Ah! we may make loud professions, but after all, the proof of their sincerity is our living up to them. God demands from us the surrender of every idol, of each darling sin, and favorite indulgence. If we comply, He says, "Now I know that thou fearest God," but not otherwise. It is only, however, a firm faith in Christ that can produce this absolute and unconditional obedience to the will of God. O! that we may have more of this heavenly principle. Then we shall be able to slay sin, to conquer passion, to resist evil, and to bruise Satan. We shall even be able to smile at death, for faith is invincible.

> " When that trump, whose archangelic peal
> Shall sound the tocsin of Creation's doom
> Thunders its challenge, Faith shall then arise,
> And firm as Jesus on the Judgment throne.
> Look on thy face, Eternity, and smile."

POOR JACK;

OR, A PLEA FOR SEAMEN.*

"They that go down to the sea in ships, that do business in great waters."

Psalms cvii.: 23.

THESE are the persons in whose behalf I am to speak this evening. Their friends are every where endeavouring to awaken the attention of the public to the claims of seamen on the prayers, the sympathies, and the benevolence of their fellow creatures.— They are persuaded, that information upon this subject is all that is required to secure from Christians the same concern about the spiritual and temporal welfare of sailors, that they manifest in regard to all other members of the human family; and it is owing to their desire to spread this information as widely as possible that I have been called upon to address you upon the present occasion.

I. You may perhaps think it strange that I should observe in the first place, with respect to sailors, that they are *human beings.*

But the neglect which they have met with from their fellow creatures, seems to make that observation necessary. Obliged from the nature of their calling to be wanderers on the face of the earth, and to spend a large proportion of their lives on the solitary deep— never staying long in one place, and separated by their pursuits from landsmen, they have been forgotten—being out of sight, they have been out of mind. A few years ago you could scarcely find

---

* Preached in Philadelphia, Jan. 25, 1846, in behalf of the " Pennsylvania Seamen's Friend Society."

in the catalogue of Christian charities one of them devoted to seamen's interests, and even now those interests are only beginning to attract attention. I observe, therefore, that they are human beings, of the same flesh and blood as ourselves, and on that ground alone entitled to our sympathies. It is a spurious benevolence that limits its regards to peculiar objects. Connected by the link of a common brotherhood, we should feel for all who are comprehended in the fraternal chain. The orphan, the widow, the aged, the sick, the blind, the poor, and the ignorant, should not be allowed to *engross* our sympathies. It is not only the necessities of this or of that class of men that should awaken our compassion, but the necessities of all. The benevolence of God, which as being perfect, should regulate the benevolence of his creatures, is expansive. It shines like the sun, upon the good and upon the evil; it descends like the rain, upon the just and upon the unjust. And redeeming love is equally comprehensive—"Christ Jesus came into the world to save sinners,"—not sinners of any particular class, but sinners of all classes; and as every sinner in distress excites his compassion, so every fellow creature in distress should excite ours. Sailors are human beings.

II. I observe again that they are *Immortal beings.*

This gives them their highest claim to our compassion. To clothe the naked, to feed the hungry, to console the miserable and to relieve the indigent, are charitable objects, but they are not the most exalted objects of human charity; and for this reason they are not the most important—the highest object of charity is that which has absorbed the solicitudes of heaven; which has excited in the bosom of every angel and archangel about the throne the deepest interest; which has so awakened the sympathies of the Son of God as to make him willing to die for its relief. The soul is the highest object of charity. What comparison is there between the worth of the soul and that of the body? The soul, with its vast powers, and the body with its feeble capacities; the soul, with its endless existence, and the body, with its brief duration; the soul, with its untold destinies, and the body, with its paltry interests. The salvation of a single soul would be a higher act of benevolence than to abolish all the physical suffering and to dispel all the mental darkness that exists in the world; because the salvation of that soul would secure its happiness, not only for the brief space allotted to us in this life, but forever and ever. And the noblest Christian charities of the day are founded upon this principle. The societies for furnishing every nation under heaven with the word of God in its own tongue, the societies for the propagation of the gospel in foreign parts, the societies for sending missionary heralds into heathen lands—they are all founded upon the principle that the value of the soul gives it a claim upon our sympathies, and exertions, and prayers, far exceeding that of any other charitable object whatever. And if so, whence this neglect of those who go down to the sea in ships? Is one soul more valuable than another, that we charter vessels to send preachers and Bibles into distant countries, whilst we make no effort for the conversion of those by whom they are navigated? Are the souls of Hottentots and Caffres of more esteem than the souls of seamen? The truth is, my brethren, that the benevolence of many is too much regulated by fancy and too little by principle. The conversion of cannibals and barbarians, who celebrate their detestable orgies before hideous idols is an enterprise so fraught with romance and heroism, so full of sentiment and adventure, that in comparison, the claims of seamen appear to be an insipid subject. But fancy is no fit umpire in this cause. The principle is the thing by which we should be governed, and that teaches us that a soul ready to perish, whether it be the soul of the barbarian or the Greek, the Jew or the Gentile, the bond or the free, is equally precious. With the strangest inconsistency men have associated for the prevention of cruelty to animals, whilst the souls of seamen were allowed to perish. They have forgotten altogether that seamen have souls, and leaving those souls to die, they have busied themselves in relieving the sufferings of the horse and the dog. I am far from insinuating any thing to the disparagement of other charities. Benevolence, as has been already observed, cannot be too extensive. We only complain that it has not been extensive enough; that whilst it has groaned over the degradation of the idolator, and has even condescended to weep over the sufferings of the brute, it has scarcely so much as cast its eye upon the distress of the seaman. Are his numbers then so small as to have caused the oversight? On the contrary, there are two millions of sailors in the world—there are one hundred and fifty thousand in your own land. Are numbers like these so insignificant as to escape notice or deserve neglect? *Deserve neglect!*— I recall that expression. If there were but one soul in danger of perdition, if, excepting one soul, the entire population of the globe were converted to Christ—it would be an achievement worthy of the ambition of all the rest—it would be a deed honourable to their benevolence—it would be an exploit that would cover them with glory and make heaven ring with the songs and acclamations of angels to snatch that one soul from destruction. Sailors are immortal beings.

III. But I observe again that they are *unfortunate beings.*

1. In the *neglect that they have experienced.*

When you see them reeling in the streets or carousing on shore, when you listen to their boisterous mirth, their obscene songs and their profane language, do not ascribe these proofs of profligacy and thoughtlessness to their being naturally worse than other men. Ascribe them to their being more neglected than other men—to the little care that has been taken for the promotion of their happiness, the improvement of their minds, the culture of their affections and the formation of their habits. Ascribe them to their being thrown early in life upon a cold, unfeeling, and selfish world, which has been too much occupied in the prosecution of its own

interests, to think of theirs. Ascribe them to their being prema-
turely divorced from the beloved inmates, the quiet pleasures, the
sacred duties, the holy influences of home. It is to these that we
are all of us, more or less, indebted for the development of our
intellectual character, the culture of our feelings, and the possession
of our religious principles. If we have escaped from ignorance
and vice, and from their accompanying degradation and wretchedness, it has been owing to the watchful superintendence that we
experienced in youth. But the sailor, often abandoning his home
whilst yet a child, is often abandoned even in childhood, to immoral
influences. He hears what? a mother's prayers? a mother's coun-
sels? a father's admonitions? a father's warnings? No. He hears
sacred things ridiculed, religion laughed at, vice applauded, and the
name of God blasphemed. He hears it from stem to stern, in the
steerage and in the forecastle, and too often on the quarter deck.
Instead of seeing the highest principles and best feelings of our
nature exemplified in those who are his shipmates and constant
associates, he too often has nothing before his eyes but the example
of hardened, profligate and abandoned men. There is enough of
vice on shore; but there you can get out of the hearing and away
from the influence of what is evil. You can choose your comrades
from the good and virtuous; but cooped up within the narrow
confines of a ship the sailor must be a willing or unwilling witness
of all its scenes, and be content with, perhaps, the worst companions.
Let me ask you, then, is it wonderful that he should be intemperate,
prodigal, dissolute and profane? No pains have been taken until
lately to make him otherwise. On shore you have schools for the
ignorant, libraries for the young, lyceums for the apprentice, insti-
tutes for the mechanic. You have lectures on science, lectures on
religion, religious teachers, religious services and public opinion.
All contribute to protect the morals, to enlighten the minds and to
form the principles of men on shore.

You have not only societies to prevent vice, but to reform the vicious—to reclaim the inebriate, and to bring back the wanderer into the paths of virtue—but, until lately, no attempt has been made either to instruct or reform the sailor. He has been left to sink deeper and deeper into the slough of profligacy, the subject of everybody's abuse, but of nobody's compassion—reviled by all, aided by none. And this cruel indifference has made him reckless. Not respected by others, he has lost respect for himself—treated as a proscribed person, an outcast, he has abandoned himself to what he considers his fate, and losing all sense of shame, has wrought iniquity with greediness.

I repeat, therefore, that sailors are unfortunate beings. They have been like ships foundering at sea, many a sail in sight, without any of them having humanity enough to lend him assistance—like drowning mariners, for whom nobody would take the trouble to lower a boat. What do I see? A vessel in distress—without aid her loss is certain, and the crew accordingly yield to despair. Such has been the effect of the indifference of the public to seamen's interests; it has made them desperate. But see! help arrives, and the scene changes; the crew work with animation and hope, their prospects brighten, their damages are repaired, and soon they are in a condition to move onward. And the effect of such societies as that I advocate has been to encourage sailors to labour in the work of their own salvation. Were you to read their reports, you would find that sailors appreciate and second the exertions that are made in their behalf—that wherever churches are built for them they will attend; that wherever ministers will visit them they will listen; that they receive tracts and other religious books with joy; and that they look upon the holy Scriptures as a more valuable guide than the compass by which they steer, or than the chart by which they sail—and there has been a corresponding result. He who

accompanies the employment of his appointed means with his promised blessing, has already crowned the efforts of these societies
with astonishing success. Many from the abundance of the sea
have been converted unto God; and as a necessary consequence,
reclaimed from vice. It is a sacred truth, that the readiest way of
amending a man's temporal condition is by exalting his spiritual.
Religion is followed by a train of attendant blessings, a glorious
procession;—she is clothed in white, the emblem of purity; a
single flower, the well-known symbol of innocence and loveliness,
adorns her hair; and, as she advances, she extends her inviting
hand to all. Temperance follows; she bears a goblet of pure water,
clear as crystal, and sparkling as the gem—her eye is radiant
with life, her cheek blooming with health—her form active, and
her step buoyant. Chastity follows, leaning upon the arm of Virtue
—her figure concealed by an ample veil, and her eyes cast upon
the ground. Domestic Happiness follows. She is represented by a
lovely woman, giving one hand to her husband, and leading her
child by the other. Industry and Abundance bring up the train—
the one looks cheerful and contented, the other merry and joyous.
She has golden wheat ears around her brow, and a green girdle
about her waist. Fruits and flowers are in her right hand, "and
in her left hand riches and honour." By their exertions for the
spiritual welfare of seamen, these societies have in numberless
instances put them in possession of these blessings, have made the
intemperate sober, the sensual chaste, the imprudent thrifty, the
idle industrious, and thus have brought happiness and prosperity to
many households. Oh, brethren! assist in the prosecution of such
a work as this, and then sailors will be no longer unfortunate.

2. But again, they are unfortunate in the *hardships they endure*
and the *dangers they encounter.*

For months, and perhaps even for years, they are estranged from
the comforts, the blessings, and the endearments of home—the boy

from his mother, the husband from his wife, the father from his children. The boy dreams of home—there are spread before him the play-grounds of his childhood; he sees the very cottage where he was born—it is embosomed in trees; the rose, the jessamine, and the honeysuckle, entwine with their intermingled sweets its trellised porch; he sees the mother he adores, the brothers and sisters he loves, but he no sooner tries to clasp them in his arms, than behold it is a dream!

The husband dreams—the voyage is ended, the harbour gained, the anchor dropped, the sails furled, the crew dismissed, and he hastens upon the wings of affection to his dwelling. He knocks impatiently—who opens the door? One whom he loves as his own soul. He hears her exclamation of delight, he sees her eyes flash with joy—but he no sooner would fold her to his heart, than behold it is a dream!

The father dreams—his family are assembled in the accustomed room, his children are there—his wife is there—he is seen—his little one holds out his hands for his embrace—and the glad cry of recognition comes from all—but he would no sooner impress the longed-for kiss upon his infant's brow, than behold it is a dream!

But separation from home is only the beginning of the sailor's trials. You are to remember that such separation often takes place under the most painful circumstances. When disease perhaps, has invaded his household, threatening home with the bereavement of wife or children. Stern necessity tears him away from their bed of sickness, and from what often proves their bed of death. He goes away, too, without the consolation of knowing that they are among friends; neglected himself, they whose fortunes are identified with his, share his destinies. They are sailors' wives, sailors' children, and he leaves them with many an anxious thought about the future. But we thank God that at least in many ports his anxiety on this head is now made groundless. This society, and many others of a

similar character throughout the land, employ those who, full of
love to God and man, visit the families of absent seamen, relieve
them in distress, comfort them in sorrow, and speak to them of Him
who is "the husband of the widow, and the father of the fatherless." But to return to the sailor. There is only one class of men
whose lives are more shortened by the nature of their occupation
than his, and those men do not work above ground. They labour
in mines, and amid foul exhalations and noxious vapours, dig out
for others the treasures of the earth. With their exception, the
sailor's life is shorter than that of any operatives. And why?—
Because the treacherous element upon which he sails, and the
capricious winds to which he trusts, oblige him by snatches to take
his rest; because he wanders through all climes, from the equator
to the pole—now scorching with heat, then freezing with cold.—
Because he works in all weathers; and because the worse the weather
the harder he must work. In the rain storm, when it descends in
torrents, not leaving him a change of clothing in his chest. In
the sleet, in the snow, in the frost, when the rigging becomes like
jagged steel, and the sails like sheet iron. In the tempest, when
the masts quiver like reeds, when the winds rage and the seas roar,
when the good ship struggles as it were for life, now plunging as
though in despair, into the depths below, and then rising, as if with
exultation, on the towering wave. Then must the sailor work;
and it is these hardships, this severe toil, this constant exposure,
that shortens his life. But alas, it may be fearfully shortened by
other causes than the wear and tear of his calling. How often, in
the discharge of some perilous duty aloft, is he precipitated into
the deep, and swallowed up by the devouring waters! How often
cast away! How often the victim of the malignant diseases of foreign
climes. How many sailors have met with an untimely death from
the club of the savage, the sword of the foe, or the desperate charge
of the wounded whale! But there would be no end of particular-

izing in this way the perils and hardships of a seaman's life. "I must appeal to the hurricane and the battle, to the ocean with its dark caverns, and to foreign shores with their unburied dead. I must call upon the thousands who have gone down with the waves for their winding sheet, and who await in the deep sepulchres the resurrection of the dead," to bear witness what toils, what dangers, and what sufferings are the sailor's lot.

We may observe, however, that sailors commonly die at sea.— Death, bitter at any time, must have its bitterness exceedingly increased under such circumstances. A ship is no hospital. None but able-bodied men are rated on her books; and if sickness befall they must take their chance. The medicine chest, perhaps, is the only proof on board, that such a calamity was ever thought of.

Where does the sailor die? In a cheerful room?—On a couch of feathers and a pillow of down?—Waited on by an attentive nurse?—Watched over by anxious friends?—Surrounded by sobbing and weeping relatives?—Far different. In that wretched hole where a suspended lantern just gives light enough to show the seaman's chest by which it is encumbered. In that rude hammock, swinging from the beam. There is his bed, and there too is his shroud. No minister of Christ stands by his side, either to awaken him to a sense of his sin and danger, or to explain to him the nature of true repentance. His wailings over an ill-spent life are unheeded. There is no messenger of love to speak to him of Jesus, and point him to that anchor, sure and steadfast, of the soul. There is no herald of that salvation which, "like the ocean itself, rises above high water mark, overtops the mountain of sin, and washes away the guilt of every penitent transgressor." He dies without comfort in this world, and too often without hope for another.— Hundreds of thousands of the bravest seamen have thus died in their berths as a dog dies in his kennel, if I may so express myself, for want of religious instruction and religious books and religious teachers. And we commend this society to your patronage, because it provides the means of mitigating, in these respects, the sailor's hardships. By bringing him into contact whilst on shore, with the means of grace, by putting him in possession of the word of God, it makes it possible that a hope may be breathed into his bosom, a peace imparted to his soul, which the prospect of death in any shape could neither disturb nor take away. He might be swallowed up by the waters—he might be cut down in the battle—he might be murdered by the savage—he might be mangled by the rocks—he might die away from home and kindred, on board his ship—but under all circumstances, he could exclaim with the Apostle Paul, "If my earthly house of this tabernacle be dissolved, I know I have a building of God, an house not made with hands, eternal in the heavens."

3. I observe, lastly, that sailors are unfortunate in the treatment they meet with when they arrive in port.

No sooner does the anchor of a return ship reach the bottom, than her crew are surrounded by thieves in the disguise of honest men. The simple hearted sailor is to be their prey; his hard-earned wages their plunder. They salute him in his own hearty fashion, and with many false professions and flattering speeches lure him to their dens—low houses where they minister to his intemperance and sensuality—give him the bowl and the harlot—pander to his vices—applaud his profligacy, and then, impatient for their nefarious harvest, they produce their bill, which the sailor, who has been half the time insensible, is obliged to pay. He has lost in a few days the reward perhaps of years of incessant toil—the price of many a risk of life and limb. He must either go into the streets or brave again the dangers of the ocean. Have we any sense of justice? Any feelings of humanity? If we be not more cruel than death, and more unmerciful than the grave, we must feel indignant at such oppression.

There is only one way of delivering seamen from these cormorants. Give them a harbour of refuge, a safe anchorage, out of the reach of such pirates. This society is anxious to build a Sailor's Home, where instead of being plundered, he will be able to save a large proportion of what he earns. Where he may improve his mind, meet with nothing to corrupt his morals, and be always surrounded by religious influences. This is the true way of helping him in this emergency, because as it is, the houses of his pilferers are the only ones open for his reception; for a seaman would feel as much out of his element in a landsman's boarding house as wo should feel on board ship. To no people on earth is the old adage that "birds of a feather flock together" so applicable as it is to sailors. Give him by all means a Sailors' Home. In the temporary establishments of this kind, two in number, which the Pennsylvania Seamen's Friend Society now sustains, there have been accommodated during the past year 776 seamen, 470 of whom have, under its auspices, renounced the use of intoxicating drinks, and many of them become new creatures in Christ Jesus. Public worship has been held in these buildings every Sabbath, daily family prayer offered up in the household, and the Scriptures, with other religious books, given to the inmates on their going to sea. Encourage such a charity as this, and a change will speedily be wrought upon the character, the standing, and the destinies of this invaluable class of men; instead of being a by-word and a reproach among all nations—instead of impeding by their example the progress of the Gospel abroad, and encouraging by their vices the march of impiety at home, they will carry a blessing wherever they go—they will earn for themselves a high place in public esteem—they will be itinerant missionaries of the Church of Christ, and hasten that period when "the earth shall be full of the knowledge of the Lord as the waters cover the sea."

And now, if the past neglect which the sailor has experienced—

if the value and jeopardy of his immortal soul—if his numbers, his degradation, his misfortunes, his hardships, his perils and his melancholy end—if these be insufficient to touch your hearts and open your hands, what additional motives can I urge in his behalf? if you have a spark of that generosity for which the sailor is so distinguished—of that gratitude for which he is so proverbial, your offerings to-night towards the emancipation of his mind from ignorance, and of his soul from vice, and of his body from oppression, will be large and liberal.

There are no individuals in this assembly who are not deeply in the sailor's debt. Men of science, what a revenue of knowledge has the sailor contributed to your treasury, and through you to the world at large. How many weary circumnavigations of the globe has he accomplished—how many previously unknown lands has he discovered! He has enriched your cabinets with the most curious productions of foreign climes. Your records teem with his observations upon distant countries, and with speculations founded upon his researches.

Commercial men, your obligations to the seaman are of greater magnitude. He has not embarked in your service in order to determine the figure of the earth, or to observe the transit of a planet, or to ascertain the locality of the magnetic pole. You have sent him forth to do business on great waters—to traffic with the savage on his treacherous coast—to chase the leviathan on the watery waste—to bring the fabrics of the East from their distant looms, and the rich furs of the North from their frozen homes—to endure hardships, to face dangers, to abandon friends—to peril life, in order that you may be rich as princes and wealthy as kings.

I repeat—there are no individuals in this assembly who are not deeply in the sailor's debt. I see many a fashionable woman here to-night who would help to bear me out in this assertion. She is attired in the trophies of the seaman's hardihood. Those gracefully drooping plumes he brought from Africa; that magnificent shawl from Thibet; those furs which protect her from the winter's blast, from the bleak regions of Siberia; those rich silks from China, and those sparkling gems from the remotest islands of the Indian Ocean. In her dwelling she is surrounded with similar proofs of the sailor's daring. She finds on her breakfast table the productions of the Indies, East and West; her eye rests upon the carpets of Turkey, the mirrors of France, and a thousand other articles of use or elegance which were produced or manufactured in distant climes.

If, again, we are interested in the conversion and civilization of the globe—if we are engaged in the mighty work of sending into heathen lands the Gospel and the temporal blessings which follow in its train, we are indebted to the sailor for carrying into effect the benevolent design.

If we have any love of country, any regard for those who protect its trade, defend its rights, maintain its honour, how can we feel otherwise than under the deepest obligation to the gallant sailor who is continually hazarding his life for these ends.

I leave his cause, then, in your hands. Assist him with a little of that wealth for which some of you are so largely indebted to his bravery and fortitude. Add your name to the list of the contributors to this Society, and you will not only have the pleasure of knowing that you have discharged a duty and performed a charitable deed, but in that day when the sea shall give up its dead, you may have the unspeakable satisfaction of receiving the blessing of thousands who were ready to perish, had not you compassionated their sorrows and relieved their sufferings. Amen.

REPAIR THE CHURCH?

" And they said, Let us rise up and build.   So they strengthened
their hands for this good work."

THIS is the reply of the Jews to Nehemiah's appeal.   Pointing
to the desolation of the holy city, he entreated them to repair its
walls, to which they answered without hesitation, " Let us rise up
and build."   It is a great encouragement to a minister of the gospel
when his plans for promoting the interests of the Church are
responded to with promptitude.   When his exertions are second-
ed by his people he feels emboldened to prosecute his designs
with increased vigour.   He interprets their readiness to abet his
views as an evidence of his usefulness, and as an omen propitious
for his future ministry.   Such are my own feelings in view of the
kind reception which the proposal to repair the church has so far
met with.   A few persons have contributed already upwards of
five thousand dollars for this object, but it cannot be accomplished
without the combined exertions of the entire parish ; and if I can
interest others in the subject, if I can secure the assistance of those
who if inclined, are abundantly able to conclude the enterprize, I
feel I shall have done for the church an essential service.

With this view I propose to glance at the early history of this
parish, for its historical associations are such, that a man may well
feel an honest pride in belonging to it, and a deep interest in its

prosperity. It was founded in the reign of George the Second, a period which was any thing but favourable to its rapid growth, since the Church of England at that period, was not the affectionate, and nursing mother of her colonial churches that she is now. A box full of old records belonging to this parish, show conclusively that it is much more indebted to the piety, zeal, and self-relying exertions of its own members, than to the aid of the mother church. The Christian Knowledge Society, and the Society for the Propagation of the Gospel, were the only means in those days whereby the Church of England exerted herself for the benefit of souls in other lands. She had no missionaries in what strictly speaking, were heathen countries. Her members did not devote their money, and time, and prayers, as now, to the spread of the Gospel, the circulation of the Scriptures, and the conversion of the world. She was like a spring so reduced by drought, as to be a standing pool, rather than a fountain of living waters. Slow, and scanty, were the streams which flowed from her hither in the reign of George the Second. She neglected the education even of her own children, and was regardless of the midnight ignorance, and irreligious condition, of extensive districts of England itself. Vital religion indeed had declined even among the enemies of the Church of England. Doddridge and Watts, it is true lived at this period, but the great majority of non-episcopal preachers, were very different from those of the Commonwealth. They were not all doctrinally sound, and of those who were, most were wofully cold. I have no doubt that the descendants of the Puritans in Newark, had more of the old fire which lived in Cromwell's time, than their cotemporary brethren in England. The recollection that their lot here was owing to the persecution of their forefathers, would maintain in them a zeal for religion, which the toleration enjoyed by Dissenters in England from the time of the landing of the Prince of Orange, did much to extinguish; for all history testifies, that religion in the camp, is hardier than religion on the couch, and that martyrs and reformers were never reared but amid difficulties. The early strug-gles of this parish were in great measure owing to the lethargy of the Church of England. There would probably have been a church here long before 1743 otherwise. The Propagation Society did not employ missionaries enough to supply the wants of the people. Their visits were few, and far between, owing to their services being distributed among various places. The Episcopalians of Newark, complained of this bitterly to the Society. They said that for some years before 1736 they had been favoured with visits from missionaries; but that their other duties prevented their com-ing to Newark as often as was desirable. And yet, there were one hundred and twenty-eight Episcopalians in Newark at that time. The people asked for a settled minister. They could not take their children to Elizabethtown for baptism. They thought their numbers entitled them to a clergyman, and they declared their willingness to contribute to his support. But still, to this application in 1736, there was no reply up to May, 1739. Make allowance as you will, for the long voyages and slow ships of those days, you must admit that had the missionary spirit of the Nineteenth century existed in the Eighteenth, the earnest and moving solicitations of your church ancestors for help for their spiritual necessities, would have met from the Society with speedier attention. Still, if cast down, these zealous men were not by this long neglect reduced to despair. They memorialized the Society again, and after three or four years more had elapsed without their petition being granted, they sub-scribed for a church building in 1742, and erected it in the follow-ing year. The highest subscription amounted to 300 dollars, and the lowest to one dollar. There was one subscription of 300, and one of 150 dollars, but there were 175 subscribers, so that almost every Episcopalian in the place must have contributed to this object. Having now provided themselves with a place of worship, they went further. They chose a candidate for orders to be their curate, and sent him to England for ordination. Unable to get help from others, they determined to help themselves. They paid his passage, gave him what is called a title for orders to the Bishop of London, and pledged his salary to him from the time he became a clergyman.— Was not this a striking proof of their determination of character, and conscientious attachment to Episcopacy? These men were in earnest. They were mostly tillers of the ground, and their chief wealth consisted in cattle; and yet they found time, and money, and labour, to bring this parish into a vigorous existence, notwithstanding the comparative apathy of the mother church, and other difficulties which I intend to mention. Do you not owe an unpaid debt of gratitude to that noble host of which Col. Josiah Ogden was the standard bearer? We want parochial enthusiasm in Trinity. We care little for what is called the pride of ancestry, but of such men as your parish ancestors you may well be proud. A little more of that feeling would do you honour, and cause you to esteem it a privilege to perpetuate to future generations, the blessed results of their self-denying labours. The first men of the parish built a church suited to the age in which they lived. A humble structure. Sheep grazed at its door, and while the pastor fed his flock within, the shepherd tended his without. For sixty-seven years this building sufficed for the congregation, but what did they do when their numbers increased? Did they shrink from the idea of displacing the time-honoured sanctuary which their fathers had raised with so much toil, expense, and anxiety, and in which voices so dear to them had worshipped the Almighty? Instead of that, they considered that their best way of repaying the large obligations which they owed to their ancestors for their church privileges, was to impart to others, what had been imparted to themselves, and to erect what compared to the first, was a splendid edifice. This no doubt was a painful sacrifice, a much greater one than would be involved by the slight alteration to gain room which is here contemplated. Here it is only the improvement of the old church that is thought of, but there, the old church was taken away, and another substituted.— There is a Jewish Synagogue in Prague which has not been swept, they say for a thousand years, through fear of sacrilege, and surely it is alike superstitious not to repair a church when necessary, out of regard for its antecedents. I have called Col. Josiah Ogden the standard bearer of the old parish, but if his secession from Presbyterianism only occurred in 1732, we must remember that an Episcopal congregation assembled in Newark in 1720. We must remember that the officers of government, some of whom resided hereabouts, belonged almost as a matter of course to the Church of England. Col. Ogden was an important acquisition. By his wealth and influence he was of the greatest use in organizing the parish, but the materials were ready to his hand, and needed only consolidation. The rector elect sent to England for ordination, sailed in October, 1743. The parish are anxiously awaiting his return. Now they thought their difficulties were vanquished; they shall have a minister of their own, and be independent in future of itinerant services. None of these joyful anticipations were realized. In January 1744 the vestry were apprized of the decease of their expected clergyman, and again they were thrown into a sea of troubles. Still their patience and courage were unimpaired, and on the very day when the sad tidings reached them of Mr. Checkly's death, they invited the Rev. Isaac Brown to the rectorship. As he continued thirty-three years with them, I shall say no more of their difficulties in obtaining a minister.

II.—But they had other difficulties to struggle with. Seventy-five years before they built a church, the first settlers of Newark came from Connecticut. This was in 1668; and as Charles the Second ascended the throne in 1648, these first settlers left England with their dislike of Episcopacy exasperated by a fresh recollection of the days of Laud. Some of them perhaps had fought under Cromwell, Fairfax, Ireton, Fleetwood, or Desborough. Accessions to their number were made, Dr. McWhorter says, by the persecutions of Charles 2d.—It is not likely that many of the original stock were living in 1743; but we can easily understand that their posterity would inherit all the animosity, prejudice, and detestation of their forefathers to the Church of England, and it was among these people, in the teeth of all their opposition, and in spite of their hostility, that this Church was established. There is a record which tells us that the first missionaries in Newark, were obliged to hold conferences and disputations on the question of Episcopacy in private houses, and there is a letter in which the writers "acknowledge that for a long time they had themselves been disaffected to the Episcopal Church, on account of the strong prejudices or prepossessions which they were bred, and trained up in by the respective pastors and teachers in the Congregational and Presbyterian way, who all along represented the Church of England and her worship as superstitious, popish, and idolatrous." —It is impossible to deny, that for a handful of men to build an Episcopal Church in a community of the immediate descendants of the Puritans was no easy task. Their enemies paid no regard to our standards. To them, a Liturgy was an abomination, however scriptural. Had not their ancestors been fined and imprisoned for rejecting the Prayer Book? They judged our Church by the traditions of their fathers, and not by her doctrines. Imagine how they must have derided, ridiculed, and taunted the adherents in Newark of this obnoxious system. Of this there is mention made in the letters of Churchmen to their friends in England. To convince such men that the profligacy of the court of Charles I., and the arbitrary administration of Archbishop Laud, were not the fruits of the Church they ruled over, was a difficult task. To persuade them even to listen to any arguments in favour of the Church, would I think, be difficult. Had they not been told that in Charles's time, " Preaching and lecturing were depreciated, and forms and ceremonies exalted. That candlesticks, and crosses, and all manner of popish ornaments were introduced into some of our churches?" The missionaries here must have had many a conference, before they could bring such people to understand, and recognize the distinction between the way in which a Church is administered and the Church itself. As for Episcopacy, a fierce pamphlet war raged here on that subject; which ended by some leading men declaring "themselves dissatisfied with the Presbyterian form of Church government," and embracing Episcopacy; and twenty years after Mr. Brown took charge of the parish, he had sixty-four communicants, a number which shows how hard a soil this was to cultivate.

III.—Again, we owe a debt of gratitude to God, for inclining the hearts of plain, poor and hard-working men here even to think of such a thing as building an Episcopal church. It is amazing, when you observe the amount of their subscriptions, and the evident sacrifice of time and labour as well as money, which it cost some of them. Mechanics gave their contribution in work. Labourers did the same. We read of their going into the swamps for poles for scaffolding, and into the forests for timber. But what is more wonderful, is that that they should care about having a church at all in an age when religion in the Church of England had sunk very low. This was not even an age like that of Laud, when there was a war be-

tween a ceremonial and spiritual worship. Men cared for none of
these things. A general indifference to religion had succeeded, by
way of reaction as it were, to the hot disputes and polemical strifes
of the days preceding the Georges. I need only mention the great
men, the representatives of that age, to show you my meaning.—
Anthony Collins, Lord Bolingbroke, Toland Tindal, all infidel writers,
were of that period. Sterne, Swift, Fielding and Smollet, all immoral writers, were then living. The eminent divines of the Church
of England contended for Christianity rather with carnal weapons,
than with those taken from the arsenal of heaven. They were good
and mighty men it is true, but "they could not see that without
the direct preaching of the essential doctrines of Christ's gospel,
their labours were all in vain." Now, if you consider the books
which sold in that age as indicating the prevailing tastes of the
people, you will understand what I mean by calling it an age of
indifferentism to religion. "The vast majority of sermons," Blair's
among the number, "were moral essays, utterly devoid of anything.
calculated to awaken, convert, save, or sanctify souls." And yet,
in this remote and then untamed wilderness, a handful of Churchmen, full of zeal and piety, were straining every nerve to build
themselves a church. The Puritan element around them could do
them no harm. What fault could their Presbyterian neighbours find
with the Prayer Book ? Many of them, when they found the scriptural character of our services, and that the cardinal truths of the
Gospel were taught in them, became Episcopalians themselves; and
on the other hand, who can doubt that the evangelical character of
this parish, the character it has always maintained for adhering
closely to the spirit, as well as formularies of our beloved Church,
was partly owing to the consciousness that the strict and scrupulous
eye of the Puritan was resting on them. "Truly this was the
Lord's doing, and it is marvellous in our eyes." May what are

called evangelical views, ever prevail in this parish. They were the views of the Reformers, by whom the Church we sprang from was founded. They are the only views which agree with the Liturgy and Articles of our beloved Church, and they are the only true Church views. Pay no regard to those who tell you that Laud was a saint, and Latimer a simpleton, and the Reformation a failure, who praise the Queen who banished the Prayer Book, and abuse the Queen who restored it. In a word beware of all tendencies to the Church of Rome.

IV.—But besides your obligations to sustain this Church as an " ebenezer" a memorial of God's blessings, and a monument of the extraordinary self-denial, courage, and perseverance of its founders, and besides the claims which it has to your support, from its representing our theological views, *the delapidated condition of the building, is in itself an appeal for its repair.* Here also I must revert to the parochial annals. The present edifice was consecrated in 1810, but the old church stood in need of repair long before that period. It was as much in need of it in 1796, as this building is at present. Were the people satisfied that it should remain so? They might have pleaded poverty with vastly more justice than we can. Hear what Dr. McWhorter says of the early inhabitants of Newark.— " A person who could expend £5 a year in groceries, and other luxuries, was deemed by his neighbours rather a high and extravagant liver."—" The heads of the town did not live in a style superior perhaps to the poorest people in it now." What did these poor people say to repairing our church? I will read you the report of the Committee to which the subject was submitted.

" The Committee appointed by the Congregation of Trinity Church to inspect the situation of said Church, and what repairs may be necessary, Report :

That it is expedient that the steeple should be immediately taken down."—"It will be further necessary to cover the whole building with a new roof."—"It is also proposed that the whole exterior of the church should be rough-cast and pencilled." "The Committee also recommend that the interior of the Church should be totally new arranged, that the pulpit should be placed in front of the chancel, and that galleries should be constructed for the accommodation of the congregation."

It is obvious that these people were not afraid of improving their church, nor unwilling, though they could ill afford it, to meet the expense. And is it proper that their successors in 1860, should be less sensible than they were, to the disgrace arising from allowing the church to fall into decay? Can you tell at any distance now the time of day by the church clock? Alas, old age has changed its countenance and well nigh obliterated its familiar features. And the steeple which is whiter with the snows of age than with the painter's brush, and which oscillates in the tempest almost like the pendulum of the clock within, seems uneasy at its long neglect. Then look at these stained, dingy, and mildewed walls, and the ceiling so weakened by time, as to excite apprehensions of its speedy fall. Surely the time is come for the parish to maintain its well-earned fame by at least repairing this ancient edifice. Think for a moment of the mortifying position which we occupy. Fine places of worship erected every where in the town. Old ones made equal to new, and ours, standing in the most conspicuous locality, in the condition in which it was fifty years past. I shall say no more on this painful subject. It is for you to reply as the Jews did to Nehemiah "let us rise up and build." I have done my duty in following the example of that great leader of the ancient church. He has taught ministers in every age, to be foremost in promoting whatever concerns the glory of God. Their position lends to them an influence, which they are bound to exert for the good of the Church. A kind and judicious people will commonly allow the counsel of a pastor considerable weight in deciding their course, whereas if he were silent, and inactive, they would probably use it as an apology for their own indolence. I commend the example of Nehemiah to *you* likewise. What sacrifices he made for the Church of God! He abandoned his lucrative place in the Persian court, that he might aid in rebuilding the Jewish capital. His prayers, his means, his influence, were all expended on this object. The forlorn and desolate condition of Jerusalem touched his heart; and he devoted himself at once to maintain her cause. Such unselfish conduct can only result from true religion. It was because he was a man of God, a man of piety, that Nehemiah acted so disinterested a part in behalf of his countrymen. There have been noble imitators of Nehemiah in this parish. I see on these walls, tablets to the memory of some of them, and I often hear their names mentioned with reverence and commendation. These men identified themselves with the interests of the parish; its concerns were their concerns; its prosperity was their joy, its adversity was their sorrow. Considering the amazing trials to which their patience was subjected, while they were bold as lions, they were as gentle as lambs. May they be an encouragement and example to all of us, and may men of like spirit never be wanting in our midst. Such men deserve to be embalmed in the memory of all who love Trinity. They deserve to be praised.

Lastly, I commend to you the example of *the Jews to whom Nehemiah spake.* They admitted that the desolation of Jerusalem was a loud call on their patriotism; nor could they deny that its walls needed repair. As Jews they looked on the ruins of their once famous city with the deepest emotions. What kings had reigned there!—What priests had ministered!—What prophets had taught! —What events had transpired! As they thought on these things, as tender recollections rushed through their minds, no wonder that they exclaimed, "let us rise up and build." I commend to you likewise their *union*. "They strengthened their hands for this good work." They worked together. The walls were rebuilt by the combined exertions of the whole people. There was a division of labour, but each toiled for one object. As the hands of their distinguished commander, when fighting against the enemies of his country, had been held up by his friends, so they as friends, strengthened one another's hands. It is by such combined efforts my brethren, that any thing you decide to do must be accomplished. The motto of the nation should in this emergency be our motto. "Union is strength."

DEDICATORY ODE,

Sung at the Consecration of Trinity Church, Newark, May 14, 1810.

With joyful hearts and tuneful songs,
　Let us approach the mighty Lord,
Proclaim his honors with our tongues,
　And sound his wond'rous truth abroad :

His glorious name, on golden lyres,
　Strike all the tuneful choirs above,
And boundless nature's realm conspires
　To celebrate his matchless love.

The heaven of heavens is his bright throne,
　And cherubs wait his high behest;
Yet for the merits of his Son,
　He visits man in humble dust.

In temples sacred to his name,
　His saints assemble round his board,
Raise there hosannas to the Lamb,
　And taste the supper of the Lord.

O God, our king, this joyful day
　We dedicate this House to thee—
Here would we meet to sing and pray,
　And learn how sweet thy dwellings be.

O king of Saints, O triune God,
　Bow the high heavens and lend thine ear;
O make this House thy fixed abode,
　And let the heavenly dove rest here.

Within these walls may Jesus' charms
　Allure ten thousand souls to love,
And, all supported by his arms,
　Shine bright in realms of bliss above.

There saints of every tribe and tongue
　Shall join the armies of the Lamb,
Hymn hallelujahs to the Son,
　The Spirit and the great I AM.

There songs seraphic shall they raise,
　And Gabriel's lyre the notes resound,
Heaven's full ton'd organ join the praise,
　And world to world repeat the sound.

To Father, Son and Holy Ghost,
　Be ceaseless praise and glory given,
By all the high angelic hosts,
　By all on earth and all in heaven.

　　　　Hallelujah, Amen.

THE DUTY OF THANKSGIVING.*

"Make a joyful noise unto the Lord, all ye lands. Enter into his gates with thanksgiving, and into his courts with praise: be thankful unto him, and bless his name.

Psalm c. 1, 4.

THE annual observance of a day of Thanksgiving to Almighty God, may now be regarded as an established custom of the American people; nor am I aware that it is adopted by any other. For the commemoration, indeed, of great political events, all countries have days set apart in their respective calendars, but a day of thanksgiving is our peculiar and honourable characteristic among the nations. How solemn and affecting is the contemplation of an entire people thus offering up unitedly their acknowledgment to the Supreme Being. The public worship of Almighty God at other times is less imposing. It is associated in our minds with sectarian selfishness, party feuds and denominational animosities. Although men are so evidently sprung from a common parentage, yet such is the effect of surrounding influence, that even among the inhabitants of the same country we find creeds so various as almost to induce the belief that there was a separate Adam and Eve for each sect. God is accordingly worshipped on most occasions, rather as the God of mountains and plains, and rivers, than as the God of the human race. But we worship Him to-day as " the father of us all."

---

* Preached at St. Thomas's Church, New York, Thursday, Nov. 23, 1853.

Our common brotherhood is recognized, our common obligations are confessed, our common dependence is admitted, and our praise no longer uttered by discordant tongues, harmoniously unite in the ancient song, " Make a joyful noise unto the Lord all ye lands. Enter into His gates with thanksgiving, and into His courts with praise."

1. The duty of thanksgiving arises from *the nature of man*. It is the expression of gratitude. Suppose, my friends, that when God created Adam, he had neither given him a heart to feel, nor a tongue to speak, could he have claimed from a man in such a case the language and sentiments of gratitude? He would have produced a being as incapable of acknowledging his power and goodness as the beasts which roamed the groves of paradise. But it is fortunate that it is otherwise; that man is intensely susceptible of attachment to his benefactor; that his affections respond to kindness like harpstrings to the touch; that he has feelings of admiration for the beautiful, and feelings of awe for the sublime Being thus qualified to be grateful, that he ought to be so is sufficiently apparent, because God intimates by the nature of his gifts, how he would have them employed. The design of our affections is as plain as that of our limbs, and it would be as absurd to say that a man with a heart was not intended to feel, as that a man with feet was not intended to walk. Another proof that the duty of thanksgiving arises from the nature of man, may be found in the common consent of mankind. Why do we expect it from the object of our benevolence? From brutes it is unlooked for. The spectators were amazed when upon the Roman amphitheatre he who had extracted a thorn from a lion's foot was spared and recognized. But in man the *absence* of gratitude astonishes us as much as its *presence* in a brute, because it is in accordance with the constitution of his nature to be grateful.

Even among barbarians the obligations imposed upon them by kindness are religiously observed. See how the Arab or the Indian will protect his friend! The lapse of time—the threats of enemies—the risk of life cannot make them forget his benefits. They will give all they possess to save him from the torture or the stake. And yet all this is done by the light of nature. Some nations have classed ingratitude with murder, and punished it with death. In short, there is no crime on earth more universally detested, more reluctantly confessed, or more bitterly inveighed against. "Ingratitude is monstrous," says the dramatist, and the death of Cæsar, he tells us, was caused less by the stroke of the assassin, than by the ingratitude of Brutus; for

"When the noble Cæsar saw *him* stab,
Ingratitude, more strong than traitors' arms,
Quite vanquished him. Then burst his mighty heart."

2. Another truth, also, must be attended to in regard to gratitude. The warmth of its expression should always be proportioned to *the amount of our obligations.* The subject matter of our present thanksgivings are the mercies of God. And what kindnesses between man and man can compare with these in number and magnitude? The world literally groans beneath the burden of his gifts, and this is continually accumulating by fresh donations.— They are not only conferred daily but momentarily. Every pulsation of life for example is equivalent to its original gift. We owe God, therefore, as many lives as we draw breaths. Every moment by preserving our life he bestows upon us the innumerable blessings which life involves. Can our gratitude be too profound, or our praises of such a Being too loud? There are thousands in the world, however, who return thanks for the least benefit which man bestows, and yet receive the richest gifts from their Creator without acknowledgment. So long as their benefactor is man, their grati-

tude rises with their obligations; but when claimed by the transcendantly higher obligations which they owe to God, it falls to zero. Some say that this is owing to the fact that by the continual recurrence of his gifts they lose their force. I know that the intensity of light diminishes in proportion to its removal from the sun. I know that heat decreases as you travel from its source; but I have yet to learn that there is a point where gratitude is extinguished by the very means calculated to set it on fire.

Is gratitude blunted by the repetition of kindness between man and man, or do we not look that men who are overwhelmingly obliged, should be overwhelmingly grateful? If because God is always giving, we withhold our thanks, then the very cause of gratitude to a fellow creature is assigned for ingratitude to our Creator. Some men there are, too, in the world, who only praise God for what he is *not* always giving, for what he rarely gives, and gives to few, such as wealth and eminence. Their mercury is always at the freezing point except on the application of boiling heat. The common benefits of God, though the most important and valuable, cannot raise it an inch. Now this is unnatural. As the glass rises and rises with the heat, so should the temperature of gratitude with our obligations; and that its culminating point should be the Great Being whose gifts admit of no comparison with any other, is manifest. Thanksgiving from man to man is a lower duty than thanksgiving from man to God. Whilst the feelings and affections of the heart respond to kindness from below, they should ascend to kindness from above; like the oak whose lower branches may touch the ground whilst its upper ones climb to heaven.

Among our grounds of thanksgiving *are the character and perfection of God*. The respect and admiration justly claimed by any being depend upon the degree in which he possesses corresponding excellence. For instance, a being with reason is entitled to more regard than an irrational animal, and a man of talent and virtue to more regard than a dunce or profligate. Every one, in short, has a right to that place in our esteem which he deserves. Now, on this ground, we cannot without injustice withhold from God our highest praises and warmest affections. As a divine being, He is a being of superior nature to all others, for that nature belongs to God alone. The nature of man is common to the human race: the nature of angels is shared by the heavenly host; but the nature of God is peculiar to himself. Beside himself, all other beings are finite, created, dependent, and mutable. We owe to Him on this account, therefore, the whole honour, and the undivided regard, which belong to the only Being thus distinguished. The respect due to a reasonable being is due as much to one as to another, and must be equally divided among the human family; but that which the Divine Being claims, since there is but one, is wholly and undividably his own. In the same way, the character of God, on account of its surpassing excellence, entitle Him to our deepest reverence, and to that response of feeling and affection which its several features deserve. Its amiability deserves our love, its truth our confidence, its compassion our regard, and its justice our awe. If such qualities occasion us to exercise such feelings toward a loving, truthful, benevolent and upright man, how much more should they do so toward God, in whose character they shine with the brightest lustre, and without any mixture of infirmity? Now, the duty in which we are engaged, implies that we have such feelings, that our prayers and praises are the language suggested by his nature, as the one living and true God, and by his character, as holy, and just and good.

The works of God are a ground of thanksgiving. Some men there are in the world who have the finest sense possible of the beautiful in art, and yet seem insensible to that of nature. They praise Canova and Thorwaldsen to the skies, but say nothing of the statuary in living marble. But these men are unjust to God, for every artist is entitled to all the credit which his works deserve. Whether the author of the works be human or divine, makes no difference. We accord to the sculptor, the painter, the writer, our applauses according to the supposed merit of their productions. Crowns have been wreathed for them, festivals have have been held in their honour, eulogies have been pronounced on their genius, and books have been written in their praise. And yet all this is done in honour of those who are themselves indebted to the Almighty, for the means by which their fame has been acquired and their works accomplished. The intellect of Newton, the hand of Phidias, the fire of Raphael, and the eloquence of Cicero, were all from God, and the praise of the wonders which they achieved is justly His. But if we applaud to the skies the works of men, with what rapturous enthusiasm and admiration should those of God be witnessed !

The most cunning contrivances of human ingenuity, the noblest triumphs of human genius, are as much beneath the grandeur, and skill, and wisdom, displayed in the works of God, as man is beneath his Maker. Man can stretch a wire around the globe, and communicate with his antipodes in a moment; but can he create the subtle and mysterious fluid which conveys his message? Man can carve statues out of marble, but can he breathe into their nostrils the breath of life? Man can annihilate distance, but can he make a drop of water or a particle of dust? "Which of you," says our Lord, "by taking thought, can add one cubit unto his stature?" or what amounts to the same thing—can conceive how in any way the works of God may be improved? Let any man try to make that better which God pronounced very good, and his inability to to originate will soon be palpable. What a prodigious grasp of mind then does it argue in the Creator of all things, that he could beget the idea of a universe, with its gorgeous assemblage of systems and worlds; its complex laws and vast machinery. Ages passed before man could discover the law which governs the fall of atoms, and the sweep of planets; the wisdom then which originated all the physical laws of the universe, must be unspeakable. And what consummate power must the realization of these sublime ideas have demanded to produce from nothing, in such excellence that it could not be improved, *everything!* Consider, too, that the most diminutive of the works of God are as full of wonder as the greatest; that the mote in the sunbeam and the drop of water, teem as much with marvels, as the fields of space or the canopy of heaven.— Reflect that even among those of his works with which we are acquainted, there is an endless diversity, so that no exact coincidence is found among individuals even of the same tribe in the animal and vegetable world.

Although there are so many plants, and animals, and men—so many that they cannot be counted, you cannot find a single pair of them without some points of dissimilarity. Whole tribes of creatures quite different from those now existing in the world have disappeared, and the process of producing and reproducing this infinitely varied and diversified succession of beings has been carried on by God from the creation of the world till now. Such thoughts, the very immensity of the subject make distracting, but they bring forcibly to our minds the adoring admiration, and love, which we owe to God. Such works as his do indeed deserve thanksgiving, and praise, and were they withheld these very walls might clap their hands, and yonder stones sing anthems to rebuke our apathy.

B

Another cause of thankfulness are " *the blessings of this life,*" or the continued exercise in our behalf, of a watchful Providence.— Every being deserves our thanks in proportion to the time, and thought, and pains, which he employs for our good. Now in order to bestow upon us these blessings the wisdom, skill, power and goodness of God are continually occupied. He devotes, if I may so express myself, His time, His resources, His contrivance and His study, for our interests. Thus our preservation is owing to His incessantly warding off from us disease and accident—to His maintaining uninterruptedly the succession of seasons, the fecundity of the earth, the salubrity of the air and that constitution of things, which, to such beings as we are, if deranged for a moment, would prove fatal. This shows how busy God must be in our behalf; for, that nothing may go wrong, He must be everywhere and see every thing. Were He to leave the helm of the great ship that He has built, for a single moment, it must go to pieces. He must not only control and direct the movements of the world, but those of the atom, because a single screw out of place in this vast machine, might be destructive. He must foresee every danger which He averts, and have a perfect knowledge of every event before it happens. And what thanks are not due to God for such sleepless regard to our interests, and unwearied exertions in our favour !— What goodness to occupy himself every moment in supplying our fast recurring necessities, and in daily bestowing upon us the richest blessings.

For these alone we can never be sufficiently thankful. *Unbroken health,* without which, though possessing all things, we enjoy— nothing. Oh, it must be a cold and withered heart that lies within that man's breast who does not praise God for the unimpaired energies of his frame, notwithstanding, perhaps, pernicious dissipations and wearing toils. "Strange" indeed is it that under such circumstances, "a harp of ten thousand strings should keep in tune so long." There is a *sound mind* without which nature would be a blank.— There are not only the necessaries of life, but the feast, which for our taste, our imagination, our curiosity and our reason, are every where spread in the works of God. There are also *home*, that "nest of delights," and all the sweets of domestic happiness. But thousands of volumes and ten thousand times ten thousand tongues could not exhaust the catalogue. What affecting passages, my hearers, in each one's history, would such a recapitulation involve! What tales of hair breadth escapes, singular recoveries, and special interpositions! Some, God has rescued from dangers, some He has snatched from death, and some He has saved from ruin. Many have struggled hard with adversity, who are now prosperous, and many have acquired a handsome competence who were once poor.

"The blessings of this life" will remind numbers of the up-hill part of its journey, and make them think, perhaps with tears, of the humiliations and hardships of the past, but it will remind them also, and I trust make them unfeignedly thankful for the happy change which they have since experienced. All the praises which we owe to God for these blessings, His creatures, were they to unite as one man in the attempt, could never render. If we extol the charity which relieves one object, how can we sufficiently praise Him, who "openeth his hand and satisfieth the desire of every living thing? If we praise the benefactor who merely shows kindness to his friends, what admiration is due to Him who feeds his enemies and "makes his sun to shine upon the evil and upon the good?" If we applaud the benevolence which visits prisons, and improves the condition of the insane, how can we sufficiently applaud Him who liberates and restores those who are enslaved and maddened by sin ? If no praises are thought too great for the patriot who sacrifices his possessions for his country's good, what praises does He deserve who " gave His only begotten Son that whosoever believeth in Him should not perish but have everlasting life."

Our present thanksgivings, however, are not only offered for our individual, but *national mercies*. "The good that men do" is not always " buried with their bones," for the custom which we now see generally established of a public thanksgiving to Almighty God, originated with those who have long since been numbered with the dead. It will be 232 years ago on the 11th day of next month, since the first demonstration of this nature was made; by men too in an unexplored wilderness, in the midst of savages and thankful if they could obtain sufficient food to support their lives. How strange that such a practice should first take root and flourish amid the adversities and hardships of emigrant life, and that not until the lapse of two centuries, when the golden harvests of autumn wave over the thousand hills and valleys of the land, should the noble example of the Puritans be imitated, and anything like a national acknowledgment of the goodness of God be offered. What nation is more indebted than this to God's bounty ? Look at its rapid progress which makes the whole world stretch out its hands in wonder ! See the extent of its commerce, the success of its manufactures, the amount of its revenues, the numbers, enterprize and intelligence of its people ! Look at its fruitful fields, and the rich profusion of treasures with which it abounds ! Its hills are studded with flocks, its rivers are freighted with gold, and its valleys are standing thick with corn. Contrast this with the spectacle which comparatively a few years ago it presented, when but a sparse and widely scattered population covered the land ; when the forests of the West were still untenanted and its prairies untrodden, when the deer roamed where cities stand, and Indians ambushed where cattle graze. Contrast all this with the condition of other countries, where the streets are crowded with the ragged poor and the towns soiled with filth and wretchedness; where the avenues to distinction are closed to the indigent, and where honest poverty is esteemed a crime; where armies are marshalling for the battle, and where the cormorants of war plume their wings. *Peace* is ours with all its attendant blessings.

And " what shall we render unto the Lord for all His benefits?" Oh, never, never can we adequately repay His mercies; but be it ours to render unto Him the undivided affection of our hearts and the unqualified obedience of our lives—be it ours, by doing good to others, to show our appreciation of His mercies to ourselves. If as a country or as individuals we would render in any degree according to the benefits we have received from God, we must honour His laws, reverence His word, and practice His precepts. Upon this depend both the welfare of the man and the endurance of the republic. Under such auspices anarchy and misrule shall never subvert our institutions, but preserved by the restorative and anti-septic powers of religion, they shall last whilst the sun and moon endure, for it is written that "Righteousness exalteth a nation, but sin is a reproach to any people."

THE NATURE AND BENEFITS

OF

CONFIRMATION.

"And laying on of hands."

Hebrews vi. 2.

THIS is the old name for Confirmation, as you will see in the Prayer Book. Many old things, if good, are all the better for being old. They acquire by it a weight and authority which do not belong to what has not stood the test of time. The Prayer Book itself derives value from its antiquity. The fact that it has been used for so many ages endears it to us. The Prayer Book is a monument of the good sense of our forefathers. It is not only a manual of public worship—it is a Church instruction book, a vade mecum from the font to the chancel, from the chancel to the communion table, from that to the altar, from the altar to the bed of languishing, and thence to the grave. I call it scriptural, sensible, philosophical, thus to make steps, as it were, from earth to heaven, instead of leaving people to lose their way and perish, as they do now too often through sin and ignorance.

Confirmation is one of the first of these steps. Rightly taken it conducts to the next, and that to a third; so that to understand its origin, present character, and important uses, is of the greatest consequence. Let us meditate awhile on these topics.

I. *Its origin.* Many people suppose Confirmation to have no authority in Scripture, whereas it is an old rite practised by the Apostles. We are told in Acts vii., that the Apostles Peter and John laid their hands on the converts in Samaria, after they had been baptized by Philip. Philip, being only a deacon, had no power to administer Confirmation, and therefore, " When the Apostles which were at Jerusalem heard that Samaria had received the Word of God," they sent two of their number to discharge the duty. This is how we ascertain the powers of bishops—by referring to Apostolic practice. What was peculiar to the Episcopal office in the days of the Apostles, such as Confirmation and Ordination, is still peculiar to it. The administration of this rite is confined now, you well remember, to the highest order of ministers. And the way in which it is now administered is precisely similar to that in which it was formerly. Our bishops pray for the candidates, and lay their hands on them just as the Apostles used to do. Ah, you say, but it is not followed by the same consequences. I cannot altogether agree to that. It is not followed by the miraculous gifts of the Holy Ghost I admit, but I shall not be convinced that it is not followed by the ordinary ones, until it is proved that God is less willing than he was at first to bestow upon converts in answer to prayer such spiritual gifts as their case requires. As for the power of working miracles and speaking foreign languages, they are no longer necessary to strengthen the faith of the young convert, to confirm the truth of the Christian religion, or to aid in its propagation. The history of Christianity for eighteen hundred years is a standing miracle, and if any one is unconvinced by it, he would not be persuaded though he could remove mountains. And with regard to languages, the Bible is translated into most languages, and their acquisition is facilitated, and our railways, and telegraphs, and steamships, and printing presses have brought all parts of the world so close to each other that no miracles are required to spread the Gospel. Miracles may be needed to open such countries as China and Japan to the Christian missionary, and these miracles are performed before our eyes, but they are not needed to augment the credibility of the Christian religion.

You say that the consequences of Confirmation now are not the same as formerly. You forget that the miraculous gifts of the Holy Ghost were not the only ones conferred in this ordinance. Indeed it is not certain that they always attended it. And if so, what benefit accrued from the laying on of hands to those who did not receive the miraculous gifts of the Spirit? Unless his ordinary ones were given they were not advantaged by it. We conclude, therefore, that while the power of working miracles was confined to a few, such gifts as "wisdom, understanding, counsel, knowledge, Godliness, and Ghostly strength," were imparted to all. And in that case, my brethren, since they are as much needed by Christians now as ever they were, why should they not still be imparted? On this account I see no reason why, save in what was miraculous, Confirmation may not be, even in its effects, the same now as formerly.

There is another instance of Confirmation in the 6th verse of the 19th chapter of the Acts, where St. Paul was the administrator.— But the most striking passage is the text where it is called one of "the principles of the doctrine of Christ." By principles, I presume, is meant the same as rudiments—the A B C, in fact, of Christianity. I do not understand the Apostle to say that Confirmation is of equal importance with the other doctrines he mentions, but that like them, it was among the Christian's first lessons. His words are these: "Therefore, leaving the principles of the doctrine of Christ, let us go on unto perfection; not laying again the foundation of repentance from dead works and of faith toward God, of the doctrine of baptisms, and of laying on of hands, and of resurrection of the dead, and of eternal judgment." You may ask me, perhaps, since the custom of laying on hands was otherwise practised, how we know that Confirmation is here spoken of. We know it from the fact that the practice in other cases was confined to a few, whereas, as one of the principles of the doctrine of Christ, that mentioned here, like those coupled with it, must apply to all. Besides, the imposition of hands in other cases is mostly disused; they are no longer laid upon the sick, for instance, but that here spoken of is permanent. It is a foundation, a principle, says the Apostle, in permanence, if not in importance, like faith, repentance, baptism, and so forth. And then observe, that as if to indicate what "laying on of hands" is meant, it is put next to baptism, where it belongs. It occurs in the order mentioned precisely where Confirmation stands, for a man admitted to the Church must repent, believe, be baptized, and then be confirmed, exactly as these occur on the Apostle's list.

This account of Confirmation has the assent of the earliest writers. Cyprian derives it from the practice of the Apostles laying their hands on those whom Philip baptized, and Ambrose expressly says of our text that it means the imposition of hands we are now speaking of. And Augustin tells us that "though men had not the gift of tongues conferred on them, as in the days of the Apostles, yet they might have other graces sufficient both to testify the presence of the Spirit, and to entitle the act of the imposition of hands to the dignity of an Apostolical institution." The fact is, that the use of this rite has continued in the Church since the Apostles' days. It was practised everywhere up to the time of the Reformation, whilst it was retained by some and its disuse regretted by others, even of those who renounced Episcopacy.

II. We are to consider secondly *its present character*, for although in form Confirmation now is what it used to be, time has made some difference in its application necessary. First, it is now *separated from baptism*, whereas in the Apostles' days it was the concluding part of it. Most of those whom they baptized were adults, who, from conviction of its truths, had embraced the Gospel, and were of course prepared without further instruction to be confirmed. But now that the subjects of baptism are mostly infants, they are not confirmed until they reach years of discretion, in order that they may be taught the doctrines of Christianity, and assume intelligently the obligations of a Christian; and not only so, but that they may give the Church a competent proof of their sincerity.—What she requires of persons to be baptized who are grown up, she requires of persons to be confirmed who were baptized in infancy—repentance and faith—and therefore she postpones confirming them until warranted to do so by their professing themselves to be penitent believers in Jesus Christ. Confirmation, therefore, is a *Profession of Faith*. If asked by a man baptized in childhood, " What doth hinder me to be confirmed?" I would say as Philip did to the Ethiopian, " If thou believest with all thine heart thou mayest." Some deprive our services of all their significance. They make Confirmation nothing more than a statement of what we are *bound* to believe. But would that be any assurance to the Church that the candidate accepts the conditions on which, in the faith that he would do so when he came of age, the promises of God were made to him in Baptism? What promise of serving God does he make who only says that he ought to serve him? It is no more the promise than is the avowal of the inebriate that he ought to be sober, of the thief that he ought to be honest, or of the profligate that he ought to be chaste. I understand that in Confirmation we make a voluntary promise for ourselves of what in our name was promised by our sponsors in baptism. They promised that we should renounce what God forbids, believe what He reveals, and do what He commands, and to say only that we are bound to do this is not to promise what they promised. It is to promise nothing, and to confirm nothing. Some may ask, What then becomes of the benefits conferred on infants at baptism? We do not know from Scripture, in the first place, what are the precise benefits then conferred on them. We argue altogether on that subject from analogy and the general promises of Christ. And in the second place, as Bishop Wilson says, in his exposition of the Colossians, " The omission of details as to the actual blessings received in baptism at the time by infants, is in order to leave everything dependent on their subsequent repentance and faith." In other words, they are conditional upon their becoming, when they grow up, penitent believers in Jesus Christ, and avail nothing otherwise. A great deal is sometimes expected from Confirmation to graceless persons, but no Church can assure an impenitent and unconverted sinner that blessings conditional on his faith and repentance belong to him. The Bishop has no power to confer those blessings, neither can he give him faith and repentance. Unless given to him by God before he is confirmed, they are not to be procured from this ordinance. It may strengthen a weak faith, but it can never make a man a believer. But besides being a profession of faith, it is, as Bishop Hobart remarks, *a confirmation from the candidate to the Church, and from the Church to the candidate.* Not only does the candidate give every assurance of his sincerity to the Church that it requires, but prayer is offered in return for his confirmation in grace, and he is assured or certified, as the Prayer Book says, of "God's favour and goodness." In fact, this is what the laying on of hands signifies, not only a sign of goodwill, nor merely to indicate the person prayed for, but significantly to denote the stedfastness of God's promises to those who are true to their own. That if our engagements are not violated, God, we may be assured, will keep his.

III. Now we come to *the uses of Confirmation,* for after all it is not the age and origin, but the practical utility of the rite that makes it valuable. It must be remembered, however, that as part of our Church system, Confirmation depends for its usefulness on what goes before. The educational part of that system extends from the font to the communion table, and relies for its efficiency upon each of its departments being rightly administered, so that neglect in one, say for instance the primary department, the training of children, annuls the utility of the next in order. By rupturing its harmony in one particular, you mar the efficacy of the whole system. I was once applied to for baptism by a person already confirmed. To use an academical phrase, he had entered the Sophomore class without passing the Freshman. This with us is illegal; in our college every man must pass from the lowest to the highest form. He must be prepared by the first step for the second, by the second for the third, and so on. To be confirmed before he is baptized, will do a man as little good as going into Thucydides before acquiring the Greek grammar. I shall take it for granted, therefore, in speaking of the uses of Confirmation, that it is not divorced from its antecedents, that the nurture, drill, and discipline which the Church requires in the preceding interval, have been attended to.

Observe then, first of all, that *parents and sponsors are reminded by it of their obligations.* It is the goal proposed to them at baptism. It is almost the last word that the minister utters. "Take care," he says, "Take care,"—words of solemn, earnest caution. They seem to say, "I have baptized this child—I have dedicated it to God—I have put His Son's mark on it, as one of the soldiers and servants of Jesus Christ. 'Take care' that it is brought up accordingly—not simply ' brought to the Bishop,' but so educated that when brought he may devoutly, sincerely, and in dependence on the Holy Ghost, say Yes to the questions put to him." "Take care that this child be brought to the Bishop to be confirmed by him." Thus Confirmation, even while the moisture of baptism is on the infant's brow, is placed in full view of its guardians, reminding them that the religious education of the child should be the great end, aim, and object of their exertion; and they are so reminded by it throughout its infancy, childhood, and youth, all the time that it is growing up. What can be more useful than such a remembrance! Oh! how true it is that there is a beautiful order in our Church services. They are like a chain reaching from the cradle

B

to the grave. Each link is united with the other, and humanly speaking, the character of a man's whole life may be prognosticated, if you know only how he was brought up from the first link of the chain to the second. How he will act as a husband, a father, a citizen, under God, depends upon the manner in which his sponsors at the font discharged their duty. There are exceptions, for sometimes the best men have the worst children ; but the rule is, that as "the twig is bent the tree's inclined." The rule is, "Train up a child in the way he should go, and when he is old he will not depart from it." This is one way, then, in which Confirmation is useful. Parents and sponsors are reminded by it of their duties.

But again, it *improves society* by pouring into it a perpetual stream of moral life, Christian virtues, and religious principles.—The want of home education and fireside religion are social evils of the greatest magnitude. They introduce into society, to rot and poison it, thousands nurtured amid curses, drunkenness, and corruption, who live only to mislead the ignorant, to betray the heedless, and to pervert the young; who sally forth when grown up, with brutal habits, and fierce passions to deceive, plunder, maim, and even to assassinate their fellow men. Confirmation, with its concomitants, abates in some measure to society these great calamities. It converts every household, where it is prepared for, into a school of Christ, and a nursery of the Church, from which in due time go forth men and women pledged by the most solemn vows to employ all their influence on the side of holiness. Thus society is improved, if it be not purified. Its Augæan stable, if not cleansed by the waters that come from this fountain, is made at any rate less noxious and destructive. That such results flow from it in any degree adequate to our strength and numbers, is not pretended. But to what is that owing? Not to any defect in our educational system, but to its wide-spread and deplorable neglect :—to the fact that so many parents never open their lips to their children on religious subjects, never say a word to them about their souls from the time they can walk till they reach maturity;—to the fact that even among the wealthy and educated there are so many households where prayer is never offered, the Bible never read, nor the word "Church" mentioned. I do not claim these results, you remember, for Confirmation by itself. I do not impute any such virtue to Episcopal hands as to expect that a youth who never heard of religion until charged for the nonce with the Creed, Lord's Prayer, Ten Commandments, and Church Catechism, will become a saint by their imposition. No; but I claim these results for Confirmation in alliance, as I said in the outset, with Christian training. And I believe that were it so connected, the humblest of our two thousand parishes might send annually into the world men who like Washington, would be patterns of piety and virtue—with Howard light up the cells of prisoners with hope—with Fry raise from the dust the vile and perishing—with Marsh read the Scriptures to the poor and ignorant—or with Raikes snatch the children of the vicious, squalid, and degraded inhabitants of large towns from the doom that awaits them, if educated in the dens of wickedness where they were born.

There were seventeen thousand persons confirmed, and twenty-five thousand baptized in our Church last year. What a sacred and sanctifying influence, if they were all brought up as the Church directs, must they exert upon society!

IV. Again, Confirmation *is a help to the Church.* Look at its value as a safeguard against the admission within her pale of improper persons. What other security has the Church against this evil? She cannot say to one applying for Confirmation, as the Apostle did to Simon Magus, "Thy heart is not right in the sight of God."— "Thou art in the gall of bitterness, and in the bond of iniquity." Neither has she power, irrespective of his spiritual condition, to confer inward and spiritual grace upon the candidates. Spiritual gifts must be received in a spiritual manner, and of course cannot be imparted where no spiritual life previously exists. In fact, it is only upon the supposition of its existence that the Church is entitled to admit even to her external privileges. And what other guaranty has she of this but the candidate's word? Her sole test of his sincerity is a solemn declaration on his part that he possesses those qualifications of which God alone is the infallible Judge. How important, then, is Confirmation to the Church, as the only pledge she can obtain of the reality of his faith, and the sincerity of his professions! And here again the connection between the pious nurture of children and this rite is manifest. Its security is strengthened, if they have been trained from infancy in the course prescribed at baptism. Their word acquires a value from that circumstance, which it would not have otherwise, because no less could be expected from them than that when old enough they would confirm their promises. But the promise of those brought up to love what in Confirmation they profess to renounce, may well be questioned, for "Can the Ethiopian change his skin, or the leopard his spots? Then may" they "also do good that are accustomed to do evil."— What reliance can be placed on their promises? They are only confirmed in compliance with custom, and because they are of a certain age. Confirmation in that case is no safeguard. Its value as such depends altogether on previous training. Again our Church looks to Confirmation for her *firmest adherents and best friends*, because on those who were brought up within her pale she has the strongest claims. They are indebted to her maternal care, ceaseless vigilance, and heavenly teaching and so are naturally more attached to her than those whom she adopts in later life. To these she is not endeared by early memories. They cannot think of her as their guardian, preceptress, and spiritual nurse. They are noble auxiliaries; they sustain her enterprises, enlarge her borders, and strengthen her stakes, but for a constant supply of hearty advocate she must look to her native citizens, and Confirmation here is an important help. To secure this supply is the end and aim of our educational system. Men are not born Churchmen, any more than they are born navigators; they must be educated for it, they must be trained to it, and that training must be such as God is likely to bless for their conversion. The spiritual birth-place of a man is that of all others in the Lord's vineyard, whereon his affections centre, and as her main dependence, the first thing our Church aims at is to gain that claim to his regard. And what better method could she adopt, than after stamping Christ's signet on his brow at baptism, to provide for his being "taught to lead a Godly and Christian life,"—for his learning all things which a Christian ought to know and believe to his soul's health—for his assuming the responsibilities of a Christian when he comes of age, and for his admission to the Lord's Supper afterwards? What she expects from this course is plain from her rubric: "There shall none be admitted to the Holy Communion until such time as he be confirmed, or be ready and desirous to be confirmed." By this she intimates her expectation that they who have been carefully nurtured in the fear of the Lord will go on unto perfection, will become her communicants, her staunchest defenders and best friends, that her "sons will be planted together in the courts of our Lord, and her daughters be as the polished corners of the temple."

Once more, what a benefit is Confirmation *to children themselves*. Not going to the Bishop at a certain age for his blessing, or to relieve their sponsors, or to comply with custom, but to declare that they unfeignedly believe in the Christain faith, and purpose, with God's help, to live accordingly. He who thus embarks on the sea of life will steer clear of the breakers of vice, and the rocks of temptation, and the whirlpool of intemperance, and the quicksands of profligacy. Many a youth, with bright eye, and beaming brow, and firm step, has bitten the dust for want of being early imbued with Christian principles. He runs riot, perhaps, for a few years, but then you will find him in rags and tatters, working in a brick yard, or feeding swine or breathing his last on a bed of straw. Even if he keep within bounds so as not to injure his worldly interests, yet by long indulgence his habits acquire a power, and his passions a sway, that render him at last a pest and burden to himself and others. But suppose he is converted, what then? Why, then he has a thousand hindrances to a holy life which would not have occured if he had set out early in the way to heaven. Thoughts that he abhors come like ghosts from their graves to disturb his peace. Torturing memories trouble the serenity of his mind. His shackled appetites hiss like serpents to be gratified, and his chained passions roar like lions for liberty. Such a man has so many points to guard, so many enemies to contend with, that his foes, whilst he is on sentry in one spot, may assail another; whilst he is watching on the ramparts, they may storm the gates; whilst he is defending the gates, they may scale the walls. The cry to arms is always sounding in his ears, and his sword is never out of his hand. And when at last he exchanges worlds, although he does cling by faith to the rock of ages, and knows that He in whom he has believed will save his soul, are the years forgotten which he spent in sin and wickedness? Can he help shedding tears when he thinks of the opportunities he has lost of glorifying God, and that he was an unprofitable servant even to the eleventh hour?

Oh, remember, you to whom the admonition is yet timely, that

> "It saves us from a thousand snares
>   To mind religion young;
> Grace will preserve our following years,
>   And make our virtues strong."

Ah, I only wish I could awaken you to a sense of your need of restraining grace, for as soon might you expect a ship abandoned at sea to make its way into port, as that a youth without restraining grace will get to heaven. Oh! cries one, Confirmation will give us grace. No, you must have grace first, and Confirmation afterwards. Well, so I have—the grace of baptism. I doubt not that grace is sometimes given to people in baptism, but if to you it has been so given, it has been made manifest. Seeds sown in the heart at baptism, like seeds sown in the ground, come up; they do not lay for years in the earth without showing themselves. There is an analogy between grace and nature, and when I am told that grace seeds are always sown in baptism, I am at a loss to know why they seldom germinate. It is very singular, to say the least of it, that although the God of nature is the God of grace, the seeds which He sows in the earth should be more productive than those which He sows in the heart. To me it is incredible. Some say it is for want of culture, but the truth is, that where there is no seed, do what you will with the soil, there can be no plant; and I account for so few children who are baptized in infancy evincing signs of growth in grace, by the simple fact that they never had any. One thing my young friends, is certain, and that is, that if the flower seeds of heaven were planted in your heart at baptism, you ought to know it by this time. You cannot help knowing whether you love Christ, and whether you try from love to him to do his will. What are your feelings when you see a snake? Disgust, apprehension. You run away from it like Moses when his rod was turned into a serpent. In like manner your feelings will inform you if you hate sin—you will flee from it in dislike and fear. If you possess grace, it must be known to your family as well as to yourselves, known to them by your pious conduct, fervent prayers, and holy life. The influence of a pious youth will be felt in households. I remember reading of a boy only fourteen years old, who established family worship. He read and prayed whilst the rest looked on.— The others did not bend a knee. They took no part in the service, but only listened to what he said, until God touched their hearts, and first his gray headed father sunk upon his knees, until one by one all the family did the same. If you have grace, it will be known to the world; it cannot be hid. Has grace taught you your guilt and led you to Jesus? Have you given your heart to him? Is it your sincere desire to serve and honor him? Then Confirmation will strengthen your purposes, and evince the sincerity of your professions. I cordially invite all who love the Saviour to be confirmed. None are excluded by our church but those who love sin, who have no intention of renouncing the world, the flesh, and the Devil.

And now I call upon parents and others to make it known to me, if acquainted with young people who are ready and desirous to be confirmed. I call upon them to aid their minister by using their influence with such persons to overcome the reluctance which prevents so many, when an opportunity of this kind occurs, from speaking to the minister about their souls. Parents, sponsors, and all who feel an interest in the Kingdom of Christ, should try to induce those whom they have reason to think are subject of divine grace to come forward. For their encouragement, let them see that you regard the approaching Confirmation as an event of interest, seriousness, and importance, so that so the weight of your influence may counterbalance that of others who are ever ready to treat religious tendencies in the young with ridicule. Above all, I beseech you to pray that the Holy Ghost may be with the candidates, enabling them to make a sincere profession, turning their hearts, so that they may be lively members of the Church of Christ, and say, not with their lips only, but with all their soul,

> " To thee, Almighty God, to thee
> Our hearts we now resign;
> 'Twill please us to look back and see
> That our whole lives were thine."